ISBN 978-1-331-61287-2
PIBN 10212896

This book is a reproduction of an important historical work. Forgotten Books uses
state-of-the-art technology to digitally reconstruct the work, preserving the original format
whilst repairing imperfections present in the aged copy. In rare cases, an imperfection in
the original, such as a blemish or missing page, may be replicated in our edition. We do,
however, repair the vast majority of imperfections successfully; any imperfections that
remain are intentionally left to preserve the state of such historical works.

1 MONTH OF
FREE
READING

at
www.ForgottenBooks.com

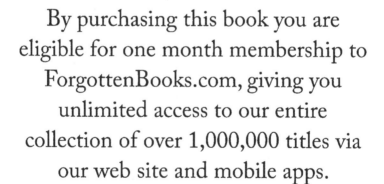

By purchasing this book you are
eligible for one month membership to
ForgottenBooks.com, giving you
unlimited access to our entire
collection of over 1,000,000 titles via
our web site and mobile apps.

To claim your free month visit:
www.forgottenbooks.com/free212896

AN HISTORICAL ACCOUNT OF THE WORSHIPFUL COMPANY OF GIRDLERS, LONDON

BY

W. DUMVILLE SMYTHE, M.A.

CLERK TO THE COMPANY

LONDON

PRINTED AT THE CHISWICK PRESS

1905

DEDICATED

TO THE COURT, LIVERY, AND FREEMEN OF THE

WORSHIPFUL COMPANY OF GIRDLERS, LONDON

BY THEIR OBEDIENT SERVANT

W. DUMVILLE SMYTHE

CLERK TO THE COMPANY

PREFACE

AFTER two and a half years of work, done in spare hours, and at times, it must be confessed, a little wearisome, especially when so many old documents and manuscripts had to be consulted, I have at length put together this little History of the Girdlers' Company, and now that it is finished I must confess to being struck with somewhat the same feelings of dismay as occurred to the small boy in " Pickwick," who learnt his alphabet and wondered whether it was worth while going through so much to accomplish so little ; but however far this little book falls short of what I wished and intended it to be, if the result of it is, as I hope it will be, to draw still closer together that bond of brotherhood which unites all true Girdlers, I shall have the satisfaction of knowing that my labours have not been in vain. In conclusion I wish to acknowledge, as freely and as publicly as I can, the great assistance I derived from the late father of the Company, Mr. George William Rich, of Hounslow. It is with the greatest regret that I was unable to get this work out a

little sooner, as it was at his suggestion and in-
stigation it was first commenced, and without the
help of his extracts from the minutes of the Girdlers' Company, compiled by him a few years back
with the greatest care and pains, it would have been
a task of more labour than ever. Unfortunately,
however, though the actual writing was finished
last June, I have not had the time or opportunity
to put it into print.

I also wish to return my best thanks to Mr.
Charles Michael Phillips, of Southampton Buildings, a member of the Worshipful Company of
Cooks, for many useful notes and much informa-
tion, and Mr. Basil Harrington Soulsby, of the
British Museum, and Secretary of the Hakluyt
Society, for assistance cheerfully rendered, not-
withstanding the many times I had occasion to
trouble him. Also to Mr. Harry Chevallier Purkis
for kindly assistance with the proofs, and Mr.
Horace Montague Prescott, the grandson of a
Girdler, for many hours expended by him in de-
ciphering the original memorandum book of the
Company.

W. D. SMYTHE.

AN HISTORICAL ACCOUNT OF THE WORSHIPFUL COMPANY OF GIRDLERS, LONDON

CAP. I

I'll put a girdle round about the earth in forty minutes.
Midsummer Night's Dream.

CICERO, in his treatise " De Officiis," lays down the following precept for the guidance of those who are attempting to write on any matter: " Every clear and rational discourse on any subject ought first to begin with an explication of that subject, so that we may have a distinct conception of what we are afterwards to discourse about "; that being so, the first question we have to consider, in a book professing to give an Historical Account of the Worshipful Company of Girdlers, is—What is a Girdler? because it must be confessed that even amongst well-informed people, and those whose knowledge may be thought to exceed even that of the man in the street, there is sometimes to be found a most deplorable ignorance on the subject; and even people who have known the Company for years are often wildly out in their endeavours to give a satisfactory answer to this inquiry. Now, the easiest reply to the question at issue, perhaps, is to answer another one, namely, What was a Girdler? and to answer that question correctly it is not only necessary to go back to the earlier periods of our history, but also to study the dress of those periods, and if we do that we shall find that amongst other articles of attire a prominent and important one was the band or belt that encircled the waist, or sometimes according as the fashion varied, the hips, and which was very generally worn from the king down to the poorest hind who lived on the land.

Now these belts differed very much in character and also in the uses to which they were put, being, roughly speaking, divided into two great classes, the civilian and the military, the simplest kind being a mere piece of rope wound round the waist and used to confine the tunic, but the more usual sort was a strap of leather, fastened in front with a metal buckle, with smaller side-straps on either side, from which hung the sword or dagger; whilst others were of a much more elaborate and finished character, being made of silk or wool or velvet, and were worn either to confine the loose and flowing robes, so as to allow freedom of movement, or to fasten and support the garments of the wearer, and were usually fastened in front with a large clasp or buckle or ornamental fastening, the long free end of the belt being passed up underneath and then drawn over the cincture, and through the loop thus formed the end hung down in front.

These belts, which varied in width from less than an inch to three or four inches, were worn by both sexes, and, in addition to supporting the garments, were used to carry the purse (hence our term "cutpurse," in allusion to the habit of thieves of severing the belt behind, and so drawing it from the waist, or sometimes, when the purse was hung from the girdle by small straps, of cutting these straps, and so taking the purse), and very often the bunch of keys, the rosary, the pen, and the ink horn were suspended from them, and at certain periods in our history, even books— they went by one common name, being known as the "girdle," and a person who was engaged in the manufacturing of them was called a "Girdler."

The accompanying woodcut, sketched from a brass in Shottesbrooke Church, Berkshire, appears in Fairholt's "Costume in England," and is shown here by kind permission of Messrs. George Bell and Sons, and is of Margaret, widow of Sir Fulke Pennebrigg (Fig. 1), who died in 1401, and will give a much clearer idea of what these girdles were like than can be conveyed by words. It also shows clearly how they were fastened, and further

FIG. 1.

is an example of a very beautiful girdle, and by studying the brasses and monumental effigies of the twelfth to the sixteenth century, many good examples can be seen.

The next illustration (Fig. 2) is taken from Stothard's "Monumental Effigies," and represents Sir Thomas Caune, a knight of the fourteenth century. It will be observed that he is wearing his girdle round his hips, and not round his waist, in accordance with the fashion of that time.

The third and last illustration (Fig. 3) is taken from the effigy of King Richard I, discovered at Rouen in 1838, and in this case the girdle is shown worn round the waist, with the long free end hanging down in front.

The best example of a girdle I have seen is in a picture painted by Mr. Edwin A. Abbey, R.A., and published, in 1903, by Messrs. Harper Brothers in their magazine. It represents King Richard II, and the picture shows at a glance the use of the girdle and how it was worn and tied. This picture

it was hoped to have reproduced here, but unfortunately, as there is some idea of
utilizing it again, permission could
not be granted.

By studying the above illustra-
tions the reader will observe that
the art of the girdler did not stop
in the manufacturing of a plain
and simple belt, but it was in the
"harnessing" and "garnishing"
of the girdle, to use the trade
terms, that the skill of the artizan
was shown, and here,
indeed, the work-
manship was often
of a very beautiful,
elaborate, and costly
character, many of
the girdles being or-
namented with jew-
els, or gold and silver worked up to a
fine degree of finish, whilst others in
addition were also embroidered in a
very sumptuous and tasteful manner,
so that the girdle was often a very ex-
pensive article, besides being exceedingly handsome; and, in the early
times of our history, in forming judgment as to a person being well dressed or not, a

FIG. 2.

FIG. 3

good deal depended on the fashion of the girdle they happened to be wearing. Curiously enough, so completely has the wearing of the girdle died out in England, that it is very difficult to discover at any of the museums any examples of these handsome old girdles, and the only place I have been able to find where, at any rate, copies can be seen, is at Madame Tussaud's Waxwork Exhibition, where there is a collection of figures of the kings and queens of England, some of whom are wearing girdles.

It should also be noted that, although the chief art of a Girdler lay in the manufacturing of girdles, several other subsidiary articles of a kindred nature, among which may be mentioned the "bandyleer," and "garters" (or "garetters," as they were formerly called) were also part of the trade of the guild, and may be included as appertaining to the art or mystery, as it is called, the details about which will be more fully set out when we come to discuss the trade ordinances of the Company.

Perhaps at this point it may not be out of place to break off for a few minutes from the consideration of the art or mystery of girdle-making, and to consider a little the history of the girdle itself, where it came from, and by whom and when it was first introduced into England, for, like so many other things, the girdle came from the East, and is not indigenous to the soil.

The first mention of it that I have come across is in the old Assyrian legend of Istar, perhaps the oldest narrative in the world; there it is related how Istar, the goddess of Love, desired to go down to Hades, and when she arrived at the fifth gate, the keeper, before he would let her pass through, insisted on her removing her many-gemmed girdle and handing it over to him. This she did, and passed on, but changed her mind as to the desirability of stopping there (even in those days, apparently, the sex claimed its privileges), and thought she would like to return to the upper regions, and on arriving again at the fifth gate claimed and had her girdle restored to her.

On the Nineveh sculptures the soldiers are represented with broad girdles to which the sword is attached, and through which two or even three daggers are passed.

Homer mentions in the "Odyssey" that when Ulysses burnt out the eye of Cyclops, the latter prayed to his father, the god Poseidon, and addressed him as "the Girdler of the earth." Herodotus recounts how Croesus, on the famous occasion before undertaking the expedition against Cyrus, consulted the oracle at Delphi, and sent there such gifts as were never before or afterwards received, and amongst other things enumerated are the girdles and necklaces of his wife. We read that the girdle of Darius was made of gold, and

that his scimitar was hung from it. Xenophon in
the "Anabasis" mentions that villages were given
to the queens of Persia to supply them with girdles,
and there are a great number of other references
to be found in the classical authors.

In the Bible the girdle is constantly referred to.
In Exodus the colours of the curious (or embroidered) girdle of Aaron are given, and they are gold,
blue, purple and scarlet, and it is numbered among
the holy garments. Gold and blue, it will be noted,
are the Company's colours at the present day.

The account in Leviticus of the consecration of
Aaron and his sons records how Moses put upon
each the coat, and girded him with the girdle.
Jeremiah prefigures the destruction of the Jews in
the type of a linen girdle hidden at Euphrates.

When Jonathan made a covenant with David
because he loved him as his own soul, he "stripped
himself of the robe that was upon him and gave it
to David, and his garments, even to his sword and
to his bow and to his girdle."

It will be remembered that Elijah the Tishbite
"was an hairy man and girt with a girdle of leather
about his loins," and again, in the New Testament,
much the same description is given of St. John the
Baptist by St. Matthew, who says, " And the same
John had his raiment of camel's hair and a leathern
girdle about his loins, and his meat was locusts and
wild honey," and St. Mark also so describes him.

To return to the Old Testament. In Proverbs, amongst the praises and properties of a good wife, are mentioned: " She maketh fine linen and selleth it and delivereth girdles unto the merchant." One of the legends of the Christian Church handed down to us recounts how the Apostolic Father St. Polycarp, just before he was martyred at the stake, took off his outer robe and his girdle, which were religiously preserved by the early Christians as relics.

As regards the history of the girdle in England, there is proof that it was in use here in very remote times, as far back, indeed, as the ancient Britons, being probably introduced to them by the Phoenicians, and in some of the early British graves and barrows that have been opened traces of girdles have been found, and Hume, in his " History of England," thus describes the dress of the ancient Britons: " The Britons tattooed their bodies, staining them blue and green with woad as a sort of war paint, a custom long retained by the Picts. They wore checkered mantles like the Gaul or Scottish Highlander; their waists were circled with a girdle, and a metal chain adorned the breast." The Anglo-Saxons too, seem to have made a pretty general use of wearing the girdle, judging from the description of their dress given by Fairholt, who says, " The general civil costume of the Anglo-Saxons appears to have been exceedingly simple.

9

A plain tunic enveloped the body, reaching to the knee; it was fastened round the waist by a girdle of folded cloth of the same colour, or secured by a band slightly ornamented." "But amongst the nobles greater extravagance seems to have prevailed, and the custom was to wear broad girdles fastened with rich buckles, the band being sometimes elaborately worked, gilt and jewelled, whilst from the pendant were suspended ornaments of different metals,"—types of these Saxon girdles can be seen depicted in the Harleian manuscripts. In the time of the Normans we read that the ordinary costume of the people was a tunic confined at the waist by a coloured girdle; but the priests, not content with so simple and unpretentious a dress, went in for something much more elaborate, and Fabian, in his life of William Rufus, says "at this time priests used bushed and braided heads, long tayled gowns and blasyn clothes shinyng and golden girdles." Among the great mass of the people however, the simple leather girdle seems to have been for generations in almost universal use, and Augustus Jessop, in his " Village Life in England 600 years ago," says, " As for the dress of the working classes, it was hardly dress at all. I doubt whether the great mass of the labourers in Norfolk had more than a single garment, a kind of tunic leaving the arms and legs bare, with a girdle of rope or leather round the waist, in which a man's knife was stuck to use, sometimes for hacking his bread, sometimes for stabbing an enemy." Among the upper and wealthier classes, however, in the time of the Plantagenets, when the fashion in dress was peculiarly extravagant and sumptuous, the girdle was seen in its full splendour, and as this was also probably the most prosperous period of the Company's history, perhaps we may be allowed to dwell somewhat more fully on the girdles of that time, and call attention to a few facts in connection with certain of them; but first of all it is necessary to premise the curious fact that, although the sumptuary laws promulgated at this time were especially directed against the prevailing extravagance in dress, and in particular aimed at reducing the splendour of the girdle, amongst other things laying down a restriction that knights whose income was under a certain sum were not to have their girdles decorated with jewels, and esquires were not allowed to have any gold or silver decorations on theirs, still, despite these prohibitions, the law was practically a dead letter, and was no more regarded in respect to this particular article of the dress than any other, and at no time of our history were the girdles so handsome or so costly as during that period. Later on, when the laws were more strictly enforced, the beauty and sumptuousness of the girdle became by this reason indicative of the rank of the wearer, and at one time it is said

that an earl could be distinguished by the fact that
he wore a golden girdle. Once more, too, it was
the priests who seem to have lent themselves to
the very extreme of fashion, and Chaucer, in his
" Canterbury Tales,' makes the ploughman scoff
at the clergy for their extravagance:

> In glitterande gold of great array
> I painted and portred all in pride.
> No common knight may go so gay.
> Chaunge of clothing every day,
> With golden girdles great and small.

Piers Plowman also rails at the clergy, and, com-
paring them with the saints, says, " Some of them
instead of Baselards" (ornamental daggers worn at
the girdle) "and brooches, have a rosary in their
hands, but Sir John and Sir Jeffery[1] hath a girdle
of silver and a baselard decorated with gilt studs."

As may be imagined, articles of so costly a
nature were not deemed lightly, and it was no uncommon thing for people to especially bequeath
their girdles by will. Thus, in the will of John de
Holegh, proved in 1351, there is a bequest of twelve
silver spoons with akernes,[2] a cup of black mazer,
and his girdle of scallopes, and in the will of
William Brangewayn, 1361, there is a like bequest,
to Johanna his wife, of all the utensils of his house,

---

[1] Priests were commonly called "Sir" until long after this
period; v. Shakespeare, Sir Oliver Martext.

[2] Acorns.

besides his silver girdle de wreches. Chaucer in his translation of the "Romance of the Rose," gives a very good description of the girdle de wreches, or, as we should say now, girdle of riches.

> The Bokell of it was of ston
>
>   *   *   *   *
>
> The mordaunt wrought in noble gise
> Was of stone full precious.
> The Barres were of gold full fine
> Upon a tissue of Sattine.
> Full heavie great and nothing light
> In everiche was a besaunt wight,
> A girdel ful rich for the nanes
> Of perry and of precious stanes.

Another example of a handsome girdle is afforded by the will of Alan Everard in 1366, wherein he mentions his silk girdle powdered with pearls, and two years later there is a very curious bequest in the will of Thomas Morice, who, besides a sum of money, leaves a black girdle with silver buckles to the crucifix at the north door of St. Paul's Church, another girdle of yellow with similar buckles to the Image of the Blessed Virgin in the New Work, and another girdle of blue to the shrine of St. Erkinwald.

The English people's love of having texts hung about their bedroom walls was also exemplified in their girdles, and it was a common thing to have texts and mottoes worked in silk and wool on the belt of the girdle. A good example of this about the same date is that of Christina, relict of John Ongham, who bequeathed by her will to Johanna, wife of John Wossall, "her silver girdle inscribed with the text 'In principio erat verbum,'"[1] and there are many other instances to be found in the Calendar of Wills proved and enrolled in the Court of Hustings, London.

During this period, or at any rate, during some part of it, a fashion seems to have prevailed, more especially for knights and soldiers, to wear their girdles round their hips rather than round the waist, or, to use the old-fashioned word, "girdle-stead," and this is to be particularly noted on examining the tombstones and brasses of those times.

To proceed a little further on, in the parliament rolls for 1423 (2 Henry VI) an inventory of the King's treasure is given, and it contains over fifty girdles, and the one which was apparently the best is thus described: "Item le seintier d'or q̃ fuist a la Reigne Jane ovec 1 pendant garnij de iiii Baleis iiii Saphers pris xi*li.* xii perles pris le pec vi*s.* viii*d.* iiii*li.* xvii Saph' & xvii Bal d'autre sort pris de chescun xx*s.* xxxiii*li.* $\frac{xx}{iiii}$ 12 Perles pris le pec ii*s.* viii*li.* l'or pois xx 'une' ovec le abatement del tissen prix l'unce xx*s.* xxi*li.* entout xviii*li.* xiii*s.* iiii*d.*" This girdle might very well come up to the standard of Chaucer's girdle de wreches.

In Strutt's "Regal Antiquities," there is an en-

---

[1] St. John, cap. 1, v. 1.

graving of a picture of King Henry V, taken from a manuscript in Benet College Library, Cambridge, and the king is shown wearing a girdle which has suspended from it at regular intervals by ornamental chains a series of circular pendants, and this fashion adopted by the king was naturally copied by the gentlemen about the Court, and continued until the reign of Henry VII.

The Tudor reigns show great diversity in the fashions of girdles, especially in those of the ladies. Sometimes they were large and broad, like the type shown in the illustration on page 4, whilst others were of quite a different character, being made of silk cord, having jewelled ornaments at regular intervals, with large pendants, and were worn loosely round the waist, and another kind, later on in the reigns of Queens Mary and Elizabeth, were often entirely composed of links of metal, such as gold or silver, intermixed with flowers, engraved cameos and groups of stones, whilst on the other hand the gentlemen of those times were often content to wear a velvet girdle, generally very plain, and in fact Queen Mary's laws imposed a penalty of ten pounds a day for any man under a certain rank who wore silk on his girdle. In Queen Elizabeth's reign too, many ladies had small books hanging from their girdles, and Lyly, in his panegyric on Englishwomen called " Euphues his England," calls attention to this, and speaks of " The

English Damoselles who have theyr bookes tyed to theyr gyrdles."

These velvet girdles were more or less confined to the upper classes, and were not worn by the mass of the people generally, and the ordinary leather girdle still seems to have held its own in their costume, and Thynne, in a poem called " Debate between Pride and Lowliness," laughing at a small tailor who tries to ape the better classes, says:

His neather stockings of silk accordingly,
A velvet gyrdle round about his waist.

In the times of the Stuarts girdles were not so generally worn, although they were not altogether discarded. In one of the Rump songs it is described how a cavalier went to pay his court to a young Puritan lady, but the extravagance and finery of his dress displeased her, and it was not until he had cut his hair, laid aside his girdle, his Spanish shoes, and his long garters, that she would have anything to do with him. Just about this time, too, among the upper classes at any rate, the girdle began to lose its distinctive character, and degenerated into an article more like what we now call a belt, as is evidenced from the Diary of Mr. Samuel Pepys, thus, " 19th (Easter Day). Up, and this day put on my close kneed coloured suit, which, with new silk stockings of the colour and belt and new gilt-handled sword, is very handsome. To church alone, and after dinner to church again, when the

young Scotchman preaching, I slept all the while,"
but the ordinary citizen still continued to wear his
girdle, and in 1685 the dress is thus described: "A
black suit of grogram, below the knees a broad
skirted doublet, a girdle about the middle, and a
short black coat." Girdles, however, in a modified
form, were sometimes worn even as late as the
reign of George II, in whose reign, indeed, it was
often the gayest part of a gentleman's costume, but
after this time they seem to have gradually dropped
out of use altogether, and can never be said to have
become really fashionable in England since.

Many other instances and references might be
set out, but enough have been given to show how
universal was the use of the girdle in England, not
only in ancient times and the middle ages, but
down to comparatively recent times, and of course
all over the East, at the present day, it is still an
important feature in the dress, and although, as
has been shown above, it is over 150 years since
girdles were fashionable in this country, the use
and memory of it is still preserved in our ancient
ceremonies, and at the recent coronation of King
Edward VII, in the investiture of the King by
the Dean of Westminster, the Dean, according to
the service, " brings from the altar the supertunica
surcoat and girdle of cloth of gold, to which the
sword is afterwards fastened, and arrays the King
therewith."

There have been many curious and quaint customs, ideas, and sayings in connection with girdles which are worth glancing at briefly, among which may be mentioned a former custom of the Jews of wearing girdles of sackcloth in times of mourning. The original badge of the Knights Templars on their first institution is said to have been a white thread girdle. In ancient Sparta one of the forms of the marriage rites instituted by their great lawgiver Lycurgus was the untying of the wife's girdle by the husband. Amongst the Romans the want of a girdle was regarded as strongly presumptive of idle and dissolute propensities, and also the Greek and Roman soldier was said to lay aside the girdle on quitting the service ("cingulum deponere" was the phrase used among the Roman soldiers), and there was another phrase in common use in ancient Rome, namely "zonam perdere," to lose one's purse, as it was always carried in the girdle. There was an ancient custom in England for bankrupt and insolvent persons to put off and surrender their girdles in open court; this custom again being in allusion to the fact that the purse was carried there, so that by this act they signified that they had given up their all, and another practice common in England was for clothmakers to pay their workmen in girdles instead of money, until this was especially forbidden by an Act of Edward IV's reign in 1463, granted on petition of the artizan clothmakers.

"May my girdle break if I fail" was an old saying of imprecation against false promises, because the purse hung from it. The theft of girdles was a hanging matter under the harsh criminal laws that at one time prevailed in England, and the calendar of letter books mentioned before gives many examples, one of which will suffice.

" Delivery of Infangenthef before Andrew Aubry, the Mayor, Bartholomew Deumars and Adam Lucas, the Sheriffs, Roger de Depham, Richard Lacer, Ralph de Uptone, John Hamond, John de Mockynge and William de Poumfreyt (Aldermen), Friday the morrow of the ascension (17 May), 15 Edward III, A.D. 1341.

"Stephen Salle de Canterbury, taken at the suit of Borewald Meausone de Dordragh,[1] mariner, with the mainour of a hood of 'russet,' a green hood, three courtepies of 'blanket,' two pairs of linen sheets, girdles, purses, knives and other goods to the value of half a mark, feloniously thieved from the ship of the said Borewald at 'le Wollewharf' in Tower Ward on Thursday the Feast of the Ascension the year aforesaid, at dusk, whereby the said Borewald appeals him pledges for prosecution viz. John Lovekyn and Hugh de Craye. The said Stephen says he is not guilty, and puts himself on the country, and a jury comes by Peter atte Vyne, John de Brigham, Edmund de Saunford, Robert

[1] Dordrecht.

Waldecart, John le Barber, Nicholas le Dyeghere, William Baret, Peter le Barber, Robert de Horsle, William atte Corner, Walter Wolley, 'skynnere,' and Roger atte Pouell, who say on oath that he is guilty. Therefore let him be hanged. And the mainour was delivered to the said Borewald, etc."

To hang a man for the theft of goods valued at half a mark would create a sensation in these days, now that we have gone to the other extreme in the administration and spirit of our criminal laws, and even seem inclined to go further, but such a thing was common at the time we are considering, and would probably pass without comment.

To turn for a moment to lands where the girdle is still in practical use. In China at this present day a quaint practice is said to prevail for the Emperor to send a white girdle to any mandarin or person in authority whom it is considered expedient should be got rid of, and on receipt of this little present it is etiquette to forthwith commit suicide, and considered bad form not to do so immediately. Lastly, in Persia, the girdle was formerly (if not at present) the cause of cabinet rank in a member of the court, who went by the name of "chief holder of the girdle of beautiful forms." Kempfer mentions such an officer among the attendants of the King of Persia, and calls him "Formae corporis estimator." His business was at stated periods to measure the ladies of the harem by a sort of regulation girdle, the limits of which it was not thought graceful to exceed. If any of them outgrew this standard of shape they were reduced by abstinence till they came within proper bounds.[1]

As regards the antiquity of the Girdlers' Company, it is impossible to say with any degree of certainty when it was first founded. Tradition says that the Company is a fraternity by prescription, which owed its origin to a lay brotherhood of the Order of St. Lawrence, who maintained themselves by the making of girdles, and voluntarily associated for the purpose of mutual protection and for the regulation of the trade "which they practised, and the maintenance of the ancient ordinances and usages established to ensure the honest manfacture of girdles with good and sound materials." It will be observed that on the face of it the tradition talks about "the ancient ordinances and usages established," so that whatever may be its date, and it is assigned to the reign of Henry II, it is probably not the beginning of the Company, and I cannot help thinking that the tradition must have originated from the fact that, owing to the strongly religious character of the early guilds and the punctiliousness of their religious observances at the shrine of their patron saint (and the Guild of Girdlers none the less than the others), many of them were constantly

[1] Moore.

referred to by the name of their saint, because all the guilds had a patron saint at whose shrine they paid particular worship and honour, and the one adopted was generally chosen with reference to some real or supposed connection with the trade. Thus the Fishmongers' Company have St. Peter, the patron saint of fishermen, and where there was no saint who could be identified with the trade itself, the Company had to use a little ingenuity and adopt one as near as they could, and either chose the name of the saint at whose church they attended, or one who was in some indirect way connected with the Company's trade, and thus it probably was that the Girdlers chose St. Lawrence, because he holds in his right hand the symbol of his martyrdom, namely, a griddle or girdle, or, as we say now, a gridiron, although I believe the expression "girdle cake" is still in use in the north of England and also in Scotland, and so the arms of the Company are an example of what is known as punning or canting heraldry, and in Strype's edition of Stowe's "London" it is hinted that the tradition of the Guild of Girdlers being originally a brotherhood of the Order of St. Lawrence arose from this very fact of having the gridiron for their arms, and to show the bad effects that emanate from a pun, the mistaken notion has got spread abroad and is widely credited that the Girdlers used to make gridirons, whilst nothing could be further from the case really, as they had nothing whatever to do with the manufacture of these utensils, either directly or indirectly.

A few facts extracted from Butler's " Lives of the Saints " as to the Girdlers' patron saint may be of interest here.

St. Lawrence was treasurer of the church at Rome and archdeacon to the Pope, St. Sixtus, and was martyred a few days after the latter in the year A.D. 258, during the persecution of Valerian. On being arrested he asked for a night's respite in which to collect the jewels of the church, which was granted in the hope of getting them out of him, but next day he appeared with all the poor and maimed and impotent people he could gather together, who he declared were the true jewels.

This unexpected move, coupled with his obstinacy as to his faith, was the cause of his martyrdom, and it was ordered that he should be broiled alive on a gridiron over a slow fire, which was done. In the course of his broiling he is reported to have said with a smile to his torturers, " Turn me; I am roasted on one side." A very realistic picture of the scene is preserved in the church of St. Lawrence, Jewry, and is most beautifully painted, being a veritable masterpiece, but who the artist was is not known, and the writer has heard it ascribed to various masters, of whom it is sufficient to mention Titian.

Many relics of this saint are to be found in different churches on the continent, such as different limbs and pots of his fat, and the very gridiron itself, or rather part of it, is shown in the church of St. Maria in Cosmedin.

Although, as has been mentioned above, it is impossible to fix any specific date for the foundation of the Company, still on a consideration of certain facts that we know are correct, and on being granted that certain probabilities are true that we think are true, it is possible to form an hypothesis.

The Anglo-Saxons were the first to extensively wear girdles in England, and I think, after a careful consideration and examination of the facts, there is good ground for arguing that the Company originated in Saxon times.

To begin with, no people who ever inhabited this country were so fond of forming themselves into guilds as the Saxons, and a perusal of the laws of King Athelstane shows that it was taken for granted that every man was a member of some guild or other.

The word guild,[1] derived from the Saxon verb gildan, to pay, signifies a fraternity or company, because every one was gildare, i.e., to pay some-

[1] The pronunciation of the word guild is sometimes called in question in Girdlers' Hall, and without presuming to give an opinion, the writer may mention that Mr. J. E. Price in his

thing towards the charge or support of the Company, and these laws of King Athelstane even go so far as to fix the amount of this payment, which was to be rendered four times a year, and was usually fourpence, which payment is now called quarterage, and is still paid by members of the Girdlers' Company, only the amount instead of being four pence is now four shillings. The originals of these guilds or fraternities have been traced back by different authorities to various sources, some even ascribing them to the Romans, who are supposed to have introduced them into England; others, again, say that in England they originated from the old Saxon law by which neighbours entered into an association and became bound for each other to bring forth him who committed any crime, or make satisfaction to the party injured, for which purpose they raised a sum of money among themselves and put into a common stock. From hence came our fraternities or guilds, and they were in use in this kingdom long before any formal charters or licences were granted to them, and in fact under the Saxon laws no licence was required. What then is more likely than that the men who made the girdles in those times (and it must have

" Historical Account of the Guildhall," says the word is often spelt " guild," but the insertion of the " u " is unnecessary, and has no effect on the real meaning of the word.

employed numbers of people, as the use seems to have been so extensive) thus became associated as a guild? especially as the Saxons had a guild for every trade, and it was often found that in the larger communities or towns it was men who followed the same trade or craft, and so belonged to the same guild, who became bound for one another; and, further, a stronger line of argument to take is, that an examination of the constitution of the Company itself affords a strong presumption that it was instituted in Saxon times, because it has all the characteristics of the guilds as they then existed, so far as our knowledge goes. There is a master and wardens and court of assistants, in all twenty-four in number. The Saxons had the same, only their court consisted of thirteen, in imitation of Christ and his apostles, as the guilds were then, as has been already observed, of so strongly religious a character. The head of the Company was called the alderman, and in the first mention I have been able to find of the Girdlers' Company, namely, in the year 1180, the head of the Company is called the alderman.

The Anglo-Saxon guilds had a rule that the whole Company should meet once a year on their saint's day, march to church in a body, pay their quarterage, choose a discreet man as alderman, who was to have the assistance of twelve other discreet men (hence the Court of Assistants), and after-

26

wards have a feast or drinking; and that is also
set down to be carried out in the ordinances of this
Company, and is carried out to this day, with this
slight difference, that under the present ordinances
the meeting need not be held on the very day itself,
but must be held within twenty-one days of St.
Lawrence's day; so that the Company's constitution bears very strong marks on the face of it of a
Saxon origin, and although, of course, the Norman
Conquest made vast changes in the laws of England, still, it must not be forgotten that William the
Conqueror, in order to appease or win over the
citizens of London, in a charter written in Anglo-
Saxon granted and confirmed their ancient English rights and privileges, so that the Guild of
Girdlers, like others, may very well have survived
the general uprooting of English customs and institutions that took place at that time, and, further,
another important fact, more fully referred to later
on, is this, that only just over a hundred years after
the Conquest the guild had so grown in wealth and
importance as to undergo the penalty of a heavy
fine from the King, on the pretext that they traded
without a licence, which they did, no doubt, relying
on King William's Charter, as mentioned above,
confirming the Saxon laws and customs under
which, as we have seen, no licence was necessary.
Therefore, taking all these facts into consideration,
namely, the Anglo-Saxon love of guilds; the know-

ledge that every trade had its guild, and every one belonged to some guild or other ; that girdles were extensively worn by all classes during the Anglo-Saxon period ; and that the constitution of the Company resembles exactly, in its customs and forms, the constitution of the Saxon guilds as we know them ; the fact that they traded without a licence ; King William's Charter ; and, lastly, the importance and wealth of the guild such a short time after the Conquest, there is very fair ground for arguing that the Company was in existence before the date of the Norman Conquest, survived it, and is of Saxon origin.

CAP. II

Sayth that she lackes
Many pretty knacks
As bedes and gyrdels gay.
          Book of Mayd Emelyn (1520).

IN the last chapter it was stated that the Girdlers' Company, in common with many other of
the guilds, was in existence long before the grant-
ing of any charter or licence, and perhaps it will
not be unprofitable to note a few early references
and entries in support of this statement, where the
term Girdler, or its equivalent, is used. But, first
of all, it is necessary to premise the fact that
formerly there were many terms to express a Girdler, according as you spoke in Anglo-Saxon, English, Norman-French, or Latin, and the following
are some of them, namely: gyrdyler, gurduler,
girdeller, gerdler, seinter, seinturer, seingterer,
ceynturer, ceinturer, zonar, and other variations,
so that it is clear that, like Mr. Weller's name,
much depended on the taste and fancy of the
speller. As has been mentioned, the first reference
to the Girdlers' Company occurs in the year 1180,

and as this is a very interesting point, and one tending to prove the great antiquity of the Company, perhaps a few words in reference to it may not be out of place.

The entry in question occurs in the Rolls of the Exchequer, known as the Pipe Rolls, and it is recorded how, in the twenty-sixth year of the reign of King Henry II, eighteen of the London guilds were amerced as adulterine, or set up without the King's licence. These guilds so amerced are described in various ways, sometimes by the name of their alderman (in which case, of course, it is impossible at this time to identify which guild is meant), sometimes by their trade, and in other instances by their patron saint, and the last is the case of the Girdlers, who are referred to as the Guild of St. Lawrence, of which Ralph de la Barre is alderman, and these guilds were all fined various sums of money, varying from forty marks downwards, and the amount of the fine imposed upon the Girdlers was twenty-five marks. Perhaps it would be as well to observe here that, if any proof were needed that the Guild of St. Lawrence carried on the trade of girdle-making, this is furnished by the name of the master, or alderman, Ralph de la Barre, as the word "barre" was a term in everyday use amongst the artizans of the Company, and was used to signify the ornaments on a girdle, and is still so used in heraldry, so that his name is an example of what was once fairly common in England, of a man being called after the trade he practised.

This fining, of course, was merely a device on the part of the King to raise money, but it shows that the Girdlers' Company, even in those early times, must have been not only of some importance, but also of comparative wealth, to have made it worth the King's while to thus impose a fine, because, although twenty-five marks does not sound very much in these days, yet, if the historian Hallam is right in his statement that money about that time was worth twenty-five times as much as it is at present, the fine would be equivalent to over £400 of our present money, so that it would be no inconsiderable fine for the Company even in these times.

The next mention of a girdler I have come across occurs also in the Exchequer Rolls, and is a licence granted by King John in the tenth year of his reign (A.D. 1209) to one Gerard le Seinturer, and being translated, runs as follows : Gerard the girdler gave two ronells of wine for letters patent giving him leave to bring into England a shipload of wine. · This entry is to be seen in Rotuli Litterarum Patentium in the Tower of London, and it is evident that the said Gerard must have been a merchant of some substance and importance. The next reference to a girdler occurs only a few years

later, namely, A.D. 1216, when one Benet le Seinturer was made Sheriff of London.

It will be observed that the above instances both
refer to rich men, or, at any rate, leading men, and
from the numerous references I have found to
girdlers about this time, or a little later, I cannot
help thinking that at no period of its history was
the Company so flourishing as between the thir-
teenth and fifteenth centuries, and although, unfortunately, we do not possess any records of our
own so far back as that date, so that it is impossible to prove this from the Company's own books,
still, in support of this statement, I propose to set
out a few entries taken from the City and other
records to show how constantly at that period the
Girdlers are mentioned and referred to, and what,
perhaps, shows better than anything else the position of the Company about that time is the fact
that in the seventh year of Edward III, John de
Prestone, girdler, was Mayor of London, an honour
that did not fall to the Company again for over
two hundred and fifty years, so far as I have been
able to find, as for a long time it was the rule that
only members of the twelve great Companies could
attain to the mayoralty, and, further, in the list of
the Companies and their members who were to
attend on the entry of the queen to her coronation,
5 Edward IV, the first twelve named are the Mercers, Drapers, Grocers, Fishmongers, Goldsmiths,

Vintners, Skinners, Tailors, Ironmongers, Salters, Haberdashers, and Girdlers, and of these the Mercers sent twenty-four representatives and the Girdlers six. The Company never at any subsequent date attained so high a place, and in the official order of precedence, made out later, *i.e.*, in the eighth year of Henry VIII, the Company was placed twenty-third out of forty-eight crafts there named, and in the assessments made on the Companies for providing corn the Girdlers were placed twenty-second. Stowe, however, in his estimation puts them even lower, and in his list of Companies, the twenty-third of Henry VIII, says "these Companies had place at the Mayor's Feast in the Guildhall in order as followeth, I speak by precedent for I was never a Feast Follower, the Girdlers twenty-ninth, four of the Court were feasted in addition to the Wardens, and they had two messes allotted to them," but if the matter of precedence should ever be officially discussed I think the Company would be entitled to claim twenty-third place in accordance with the official list of Henry VIII's reign. To go back again from this digression in the Rolls relating to the town of Berwick-on-Tweed, A.D. 1296, mention is made of one Robert le Gerdler, an inhabitant of that town, who may have belonged to the allied Guild of Girdlers and Keelmen, who flourished about this time at the town of Newcastle-upon-Tyne, and there is another entry also about the same date referring to Richard de Norfolk, girdler, who seems to have been a wealthy merchant, so that it is abundantly clear that even in these times the Girdlers' Company was widely spread throughout the length of England, and was by no means confined to London.

But, to return to London again where, after all, we are principally concerned, as this Company is always called the Worshipful Company of Girdlers, London, there is an entry in letter-book B of the Calendar of Letter Books of the City of London, which I set out rather fully, as so many Girdlers are mentioned, and it also gives an interesting picture of life in the City in the time of King Edward I, and, further, we learn from it that even hooliganism is no new thing. It runs as follows :

" Sunday, the feast of St. Matthew (21st Sept.) 9 Ed. I, A.D. 1281, before G[regory de Rokesley, Mayor, William de Farendone and Nicholas de Wynchester, Sheriffs, and other aldermen and lieges of the Lord the King.

" Bartholomew de Hallynge, John Fuatard, Nicholas le Quelter, Robert le Ster, Andrew de Kent, Roger le Avener de Garscherche, Richard Fretemone, Robert le Bere, Thomas de Arderne, John le Treere, Ralph le Treere, Peter de Honilane, Hugh le barber, William le Taillur de Colem[an Street], Adam Pikeman, fishmonger, Adam Pikeman, butcher (and others) arrested for divers trespasses, as for homicides, robberies, beatings, assaults, and for being vagrants by night after curfew in the City with swords and bucklers, and for instituting games near the City, and keeping houses of ill fame contrary to the peace of the Lord the King and contrary to the ordinances and provisions of the good men of the City aforesaid, say that they are in no way guilty of the trespasses aforesaid, and touching this, each for himself puts himself on the verdict of 4 Jurors of each ward of the City. Let there be an inquest accordingly.

"The Jurors say on oath that Thomas de Arderne, John le Treere, Ralph le Treere, Adam Pikeman, butcher, Adam Pikeman, fishmonger, are in no way guilty of the trespasses aforesaid. They are therefore quit.

"They say also that John Fuatard, Walter de Dancastre, and John, son of William de Enfield, are wont to frequent taverns after curfew, and they know no other evil of them. Let them therefore be kept in custody until delivered by sufficient mainprise as formerly was provided.

"They say also that Roger de Garscherche, Fulk le barbur, Hugh le barber, and Walter le Tailleur de Colman Street, keep houses of ill fame in the City, and that the aforesaid Roger Nicholas de Quelter, Hugh and Walter, walk abroad after curfew contrary to the statutes of the City.

" Let them therefore be kept in custody until, etc.

" They say also that Bartholomew de Hallinge, clerk, Andrew de Kent, Robert le Bere, Peter le Tabellyon and William le Coffrer walk abroad at night with evil Companions to do evil contrary to the peace of the lord the King. Let them therefore be kept in safe custody until, etc.

" They say also that Richard Fretemone is a quarreller and a bully, and they know no other evil of him. Therefore, etc.

" They say also that Roger le Lechyere and John Picard, 'barbor,' play dice in taverns after curfew contrary to the statutes of the City. Therefore, etc.

" They say also that Peter de Honilane walks abroad at night with arms.

" Mainpernors (or as we now say Bail) for Hugh le Barber."

Here follow twelve names, one of them being William Brigerdler. A brigerdler was a maker of brace girdles, belts used instead of braces.

" Mainpernors of Richard Fretemone, Thomas de la Cornere ' Seingterer.'

" Mainpernors of Bartholomew de Hallinge, clerk, Walter le Seinturer.

" Mainpernors of Robert le Bere, ' Thomas le Seinturer.' "

It will be seen that this one entry alone mentions no less than four girdlers, thus showing what a large and influential body they must have been in the reign of Edward I.

A great number of other instances might be given of girdlers about this time, but I do not propose to set them out as most of them are only records of recognizances for debt, which have very little interest attaching to them, at any rate for us in these times, but I will content myself by setting out another extract from the Calendar of Letter Books of the City of London, namely, the Verdict of the Aldermen of London, A.D. 1308, in which both girdlers and girdles played their part.

"They say on their oath that Adam de War-feld, sacristan of Westminster, Alexander de Per-sore and Thomas de Dene, monks of the said church, were ordainers and contrivers of the burglary (burgerie) of the Treasury of the lord the King. And John Albon 'mazoun,' and a certain John, servant of the aforesaid John and Richard de 'Podelescote,' broke into the treasury aforesaid and entered it and carried away the treasure and jewels found therein. They say also that Roger de Perstoke, the drawer of beer (*tractator cervisie*) in the cellar for the use of the convent, Robert de Cherringe, John de Nottele, John de Prescote, Thomas de Lichefeld, Walter, valet of Sir Arnold de Campan, William, valet of John Shenche, Keeper of the King's Palace, Roger and Adam, valets of the aforesaid sacristan of Westminster, were aiders and abettors of the said robbery. They say, moreover, that the aforesaid Richard de

37

'Podelicote' was found seized of part of the jewels aforesaid, comprising coronets, fermails of gold, girdles, cups and scuttles (*scutellis*) of silver, to the value of £2,200. And that the aforesaid sacristan was seized of a bowl and cup of silver, the value of which they knew not. They say also that John de Neumarche, a goldsmith residing at Billingesgate, was found seized of gold weighing 6*s*. and three precious stones, and they hold him suspect. And they say that Walter de Walepol bought in good faith and unsuspectingly of the aforesaid Richard de Podelicote three gold rings, and William Torel in like manner two gold rings. And Geoffrey de Bradele, girdler, in like manner bought of the said Richard a plate of silver weighing £14 15*s*. And that John de Brigeford, goldsmith, likewise bought a fermail of gold and oriental 'perles' of the value of 70/. And that Thomas de Frowyk, goldsmith, in like manner bought of Imayna la Berestere precious stones of the value of 42*s*., and likewise Nicholas de St. Botulph, goldsmith, stones of the value of 20*s*., which stones the said Imayna had received from John de Neumarche. They say also that about the feast of the Invention of H. Cross [3 May] last past, John de Uggele, William de Kinebautone and John his brother, and Chastanea la Barbere and Alice her sister met in a certain house within the Close of Flete Prison together with a horseman (*homine* *equestro*) and four other ribalds unknown, for two nights, and there spent the time until midnight eating and drinking, and then withdrew with arms towards Westminster, and in the morning returned, and this they did for two nights, and afterwards never returned again. And because about the same time the Treasury was broken into, they hold these suspect of the robbery and felony aforesaid."

This verdict was given on Saturday after the Feast of SS. Peter and Paul (29 June), 31 Ed. I (A.D. 1303), by oath of the aldermen.

A note in letter-book C of the Calendar of Letter Books informs us that Richard de Podelicote sought sanctuary in the Church of St. Michael, Candlewick Street (now Cannon Street), whence he was taken by force on Midsummer's Eve by bailiffs of the City, and placed in the custody of Hugh Pourte, one of the sheriffs. For this breach of sanctuary the bailiffs (whose names are given as Gocelin and Thomas Attwelle) were made to do penance, walking barefoot in shirts and breeches with a wax candle in hand from Bow Church to Newgate, and from Newgate back to St. Michael's, having, moreover, to walk to Canterbury the next day without girdle and hood. Early in 1304 Commissioners sat at the Tower to investigate the robbery. Ten monks and a clerk are recorded as having been charged with being accomplices, and notwithstanding their objection to being made amenable to secular judges, the monks were committed until further orders. The sacristan was convicted of receiving and concealing the King's Jewels, Chron. Ed. I and II.

The penance enforced on the two bailiffs is much more severe than appears at first sight, as it would entail their walking to Canterbury in the middle of summer with nothing on their heads, and probably with the added discomfort of having to hold their clothes up all the time because, not being allowed to wear girdles, they would otherwise be trailing in the dirt. The conclusion, too, is forced upon us from reading the above that even the lady barber is not a product of this later age, but was apparently a recognized craftswoman in the reign of Edward I.

It will be observed after perusing the above references to the girdlers that the Guild was not only in active existence, but also very numerous and widely known long before any charter was granted to it.

The reign of Edward III was a most important one for the Livery Companies, as the guilds then first began to be called, probably owing to the fact of their assuming a distinctive dress at that time, and they rose into great prominence and importance, the King himself joining one of the larger guilds, and his example was followed by many of the nobility and gentry ; and as showing the power they wielded, it became practically impossible for any craftsman to pursue his calling within the City and Liberties unless he first enrolled himself in the guild which had the oversight of his particular art or mystery, and in fact the craft guilds became very strong trade unions. Members had a vested interest in their guild and something in the nature of *esprit de corps* was kindled amongst them, so that we are not so very surprised at finding a girdler, by name Laurence Robiant, leaving by will a dwelling-house to his wife so long as she remains unmarried or shall marry "a mere girdell cutter." At that time, too, many of the guilds were reorganized and received their first charters and patents, and amongst the earliest was the Girdlers' Company, who drew up and presented a petition to the King and Council of Parliament, complaining that certain men of the trade or mystery of Girdlers, contrary to ancient ordinance and usage, garnished girdles made of silk, wool, leather, and linen thread with metals inferior to fine copper or brass latone, iron and steel, namely, with lead, pewter, tin, and other false materials, and praying that the ancient ordinances and customs might be approved by the King, and that the custom of burning all work not made in conformity with such ordinances might be adhered to.

This petition found favour in the sight of the King, and a Patent was granted in the year 1327, being the first year of the King's reign, and the following may be accepted as a translation of the document which is written partly in Latin, partly in Norman-French.

"1st Ed.III, A.D. 1326-7. Edward, by the Grace of God King of England, Lord of Ireland, and Duke of Aquitane, to all those to whom these present letters shall come, greeting. The Girdlers of our City of London (*Les Ceynturerers de nostre Citee de Loundres*) have shown unto us by their petition put before us at our Council in our Parliament held at Westminster after the Feast of the Purification [2 February] last past, that heretofore it was ordained and the custom in the said City that no man of the said trade should cause any Girdle of silk, of wool, of leather, or of linen thread to be garnished with any inferior metal than with latone, copper, iron, and steel, and that if any work should be found garnished with inferior metal, the same should be burnt, and that now the said trade in the said City is much impaired and defamed by reason that some persons of the said trade dwelling without the City, and there making and garnishing girdles, do garnish the same with false work, such as lead, pewter and tin, and other false things, whereby the people of the said City and of the realm are deceived to the great loss of themselves and the scandal of the good folk of the trade. And the said Girdlers have requested us that we would approve the said Ordinance and usage, and would grant that from henceforth in the said City and elsewhere throughout all our realm the same for ever shall be strictly kept. We therefore, such deceits and losses to avoid, and for the common profit of our people, willing to agree to this request and to authorize the said ordinance and usage do, by the tenor of these letters, accept and approve thereof, and do, will, and grant for ourselves and for our heirs that the said ordinance and usage in the said City and elsewhere throughout the whole of our realm shall be from henceforth for ever kept and maintained, and that in the said City and every other city, burgh, and good town of the realm where such workmen are, or shall be, there shall be chosen by the folks of the trade there dwelling, one man or two good and lawful persons of the same trade for maintaining the same, and making search thereon at all times that they shall see that there is need for them so to do. And if any work of the Girdlers shall be garnished with lead, pewter or tin, or other false thing, the same is to be presented by the said persons so chosen before the Mayor of the said City, and before the Mayors or Chief Wardens of other cities, burghs, and towns of the said realm, in the places where such false work shall be found, and by award of the said Mayors and Chief Wardens the same shall be burnt and at their discretion the workmen punished for their false work, and the amercements that shall arise from such punishments shall remain with the same Mayors and Chief Wardens and the Commonalty of the places where such false work shall be so found. And that the folks of the said trade who shall be chosen in the said City of London, there to make search at such time as they shall come into other cities, burghs or towns in our realm where the same trade is carried on may, with the folks of the same trade who are chosen so to do in the places to which they shall have so come, make search for such work and present the defaults therein unto the Mayor and Chief Wardens of the same places as aforesaid. In Witness whereof we have caused these our letters patent to be made. Given at Westminster the 10th day of May in the first year of our reign."[1]

Unfortunately, the original of this Patent is lost and, so far as is known, no longer exists, although there are several copies of it about, and one in particular, a clear and perfect copy, is to be seen at the Library of the Society of Antiquarians, London, and the Company also possess a fair copy. But it was several times confirmed, first by the King in 1353, and a writ close was sent to the

[1] The cost of this Charter appears to have been five marks, judging from the following note appended:
"For five marks paid into the Hanaper.
"Examined by Richard Frystone and William Bolton, Clerks."

Mayor and Sheriffs, and then by Richard II, in 1377, and again by Henry IV, in 1401, which confirmations are also missing, though, here again, the Company have copies of two of the confirmations, and it was again confirmed in 1462 by Edward IV in the second year of his reign, and, fortunately, the original of this is still in the Company's possession, and is now with the later charters and the Company's ancient Seal, the exact age of which is not known, though it is said to be of fifteenth-century workmanship, kept safely at a bank. This latter Patent, which is also written partly in Latin, and partly in Norman-French, is most beautifully transcribed, and is what is called an Inspeximus Charter because it refers to two of the previous grants to the Company in these terms: "We have inspected the letters patent of our lord Richard, late King of England, the second after the Conquest, made in these words: Richard, by the Grace of God King of England and France and lord of Ireland, to all to whom these present letters shall come, greeting. We have inspected the Charter which our Lord Edward, late King of England, our Grandfather, caused to be made in these words: Edward, by the Grace of God King of England, lord of Ireland, and Duke of Aquitaine." It then recites the whole of the Patent as given above, and confirms it.

These Letters Patent still possess half the great

Seal of England with a figure of the King on horse-back, fully armed, carrying a shield, with the lion and fleurs-de-lis impressed on the wax, and also the silken cord attaching the Seal to the Charter. At first sight the necessity for these frequent con-firmations of the original Charter at such short in-tervals does not appear very clearly, especially as they do not add anything to the powers, or make any material alteration in the constitution of the Company, but, as a matter of fact, I expect it was merely a device on the part of the King to get a fine out of the Company on the excuse of confirming their Charter, and although it may seem a little un-fair on the Company, still, in reality, the King could not help himself, he had to raise money somehow, and naturally turned to the source where he thought there was the best chance of success, and the Company had to submit with as good grace as possible and get off as cheaply as they could.

The next document is perhaps the most import-ant of all, being the Company's incorporation, and is dated 27 Henry VI (1448). It ratifies and con-firms the original Letters Patent, and grants to the Mystery of Girdlers, London, that they be Incor-porated by the name of the Master and Guardians of the Mystery of Girdlers of the City of London, to enjoy all the privileges of a body corporate, with power to elect annually a Master and three Guardians to regulate the affairs of the Mystery.

This little document, which is beautifully inscribed with a handsome floriated border, with the colours of the paint still so fresh that it looks as if it was done quite recently, proves that the Girdlers' Company was incorporated on the sixth day of August, 1448.

This power to elect a Master and three Guardians merely confirmed what had been the custom of the Company from time out of mind, although the first mention I have been able to obtain of a formal election occurs in letter-book E of the Calendar of Letter Books, which gives the names of Ralph de Braghynge, John Potyn, William de Donmowe, and John de Prestone, as having been elected and sworn for the government of the Mystery of Girdlers in A.D. 1328. Following the incorporation is the Patent of the second year of Edward IV, already alluded to, which, curiously enough, does not mention the incorporation grant, but confirms certain proceedings in the parliament of Henry V, called an ordinance for protecting the true workers who make girdles, and against the use of inferior metal for garnishing them.

Before proceeding any further it is necessary to mention that on the 2nd March, 1451, the Company of Pinners and Wireworkers were joined to the Girdlers' Company by consent of the Lord Mair and Court of Aldermen " forasmuch as they would not otherwise be able to maintain the charges of the Cittie," but there was no charter or official incorporation by the Crown made at that time, and the three arts still kept to their own ordinances and customs, only the Master and Wardens of the Girdlers' Company acted on behalf of, and were the recognized heads of the three amalgamated guilds. The Girdlers' Company is rich in Charters and, in addition to the above, possesses the Charter granted by Philip and Mary in 1557, which contains a very fine scroll-work representation of the heads of the King and Queen, and a Charter granted by Queen Elizabeth in 1567. No really important change was made in the Company's constitution by either of these latter Charters with the exception of the formal incorporation of the Pinners and Wireworkers by Queen Elizabeth, as mentioned below, and they merely confirm the original Letters Patent. The Charter of Elizabeth, however, enacts as follows :

" Whereas the Lady Elizabeth, Queen of England, etc., being moved with godly affection at the humble supplication of her faithful subjects, Citizens and Freemen of London, as well using the art, mystery, or occupation of the Pinners and the art and mystery of Wireworkers as of the art and mystery of Girdlers of her Cittie of London, doth, by her Letters Patent under the great Seal of England, grant that from thenceforth the said three arts or mysteries called Pinners, Wyerworkers, and

Girdlers should be joined and united together into one body Corporate or Polity. The said Queen by the said Letters Patent doth, will, and grant that they should be from thenceforth in name and deed one body Corporate and Polity, and one Society and Company for ever, and doth Incorporate them by the name of the Master and Wardens or Keepers of the Art or Mystery of Girdlers, London, and that their successors should have perpetual succession by the same name and should have a common seal for the affairs of the said Company. The United Companies to have the liberties and franchises, customs and ordinances touching their arts and mysteries heretofore possessed without molestation or interruption by the said Queen, her Heirs and Successors." The Charter further goes on and grants the Company power to hold all lands, messuages, and hereditaments, which it was then seized of, possessed, used, or enjoyed, with further power to purchase like land and heredita-ments to the value of £40 per annum. Then follow the clauses of the Charter which I do not propose to set out as they are much the same as in the original, only brought more in accordance with the times.

It does not appear that the Pinners and Wire-workers brought any accession of property to the Girdlers, and the amalgamation does not seem to have worked very well, as we find in the Calendar of State Papers (Domestic) in the year 1637 a petition of the artizan Pinners, Wireworkers, and Girdlers of London to the King, which recites that in the tenth year of Queen Elizabeth, the said three arts were incorporated and so continued till of late years many merchants and others, not being artizans, are become Governors of the Corporation, and have not only neglected to put into execution the ordinances made for the well-governing of the said arts, but by their greatness, assuming the power over the artizans, have converted their revenues to other uses. On complaint of the artizan Pinners, the King granted them a corporation by themselves; since that grant the Governors of the Girdlers and Wyerworkers, being no artizans, have obtained for themselves grant for the sole government of the said two lists, and for disposing of the stocks and revenues of all three arts. Pray that the grant may be stayed and that the examination of the premises may be referred to whom your Majesty shall think fit. The Earl of Dorset and secretary Windebank, after some correspondence, were appointed to look into the matter as referees, and they, after investigation, informed the King that the grant lately made to the Pinmakers did not dissever them sufficiently from the Company of Girdlers, and they remained still of that body, and they submitted to the King the propriety of severing them entirely, and that a fit proportion of the real and personal estate of the Company of Girdlers should be allowed the Pinmakers, and they further recommended that directions should be given to the King's Council to accomplish these ends, and that the Attorney-General should prepare bills for the King's signature accordingly. On this report the King ordered bills to be prepared for more effectually dissevering the Pinmakers from the Girdlers, and settling some of the Company's estate on them; so they were severed, and a fresh Charter was granted to the Girdlers and Wireworkers by King Charles I in 1640, which recites the Charter of Elizabeth as to the incorporation of Pinners and Wireworkers with the Girdlers, and then makes a fresh grant to the Girdlers and Wireworkers without the Pinners.

The present Charter of the Girdlers' Company is dated 1685 in the first year of King James II and was granted on the surrender of the then existing Charter, as appears from the minute books and under the following circumstances. Charles II, in 1684, being annoyed with the City of London, issued a writ of *quo warranto*, and got judgment in his favour, and it was declared that the City had forfeited its Charter and privileges. The effect of this decision on the City Companies was that they were all supposed to be completely at the King's mercy, and to have forfeited all their rights and privileges, and, although the question

as regards the Companies must have been somewhat doubtful, it was thought wisest to submit and
petition for clemency.

The rest of the story can be gathered from the
minutes, but it may be mentioned here, that in the
reign of William I I I it was declared that the *quo warranto* was reversed, and the City and the Companies
were restored to their former rights and privileges.

On the 16th June, 1684, the Master called the
Court together and informed them that a writ of
quo warranto had been served on the Company,
no doubt at the same time explaining that a *quo
warranto* is a writ issued by the Crown against one
who claims or usurps any office, franchise, or liberty,
to inquire by what authority he supports his claim
in order to determine the right to it, so that in
effect, this writ, in reality, aimed at the very existence of the Company. Upon hearing this, the Court
ordered the whole Company to be summoned, and
the matter was " seriously and calmly discussed,"
and finally, on the same day, a Petition To The
King's Most Excellent Majesty was drawn up, in
which it was stated that the Company was desirous
of laying themselves at His Majesty's feet, and
further, earnestly begged that His Majesty would
be graciously pleased to pardon anything that was
past, and accept of their humble submission to
his sacred Majesty's will and pleasure, and that
His Majesty would be further pleased to grant

them their former privileges, immunities, and franchises, with such regulations for the government of the said Company as his sacred Majesty should think fit.

The Master and Wardens were desired to present this petition, and it was determined that a surrender should be made of the present Charters; accordingly, a little later, the surrender agreed upon then being fairly engrossed and distinctly read over, was, with the approbation and consent of the assistants now present, actually sealed with the Yeoman Seal of the Company by the Master and Wardens, and delivered by them as the act and deed of the Company; a copy whereof was now ordered to be entered at large in the acts and orders of the Court, which is as follows:

" To all to whom these Presents shall come, the Master, Wardens, and Assistants of the Art and Mystery of the Girdlers of London, send Greetings. Know ye, that considering how much it imports the Government of the City and the Companies thereof to have persons of known loyalty and approved integrity to bear office of trust therein, We, the said Master, Wardens, and Assistants, have granted, surrendered, and yielded up, and by these presents do grant, surrender, and yield up unto our most gracious sovereign Lord Charles II, by the Grace of God of England, Scotland, France, and Ireland, King Defender of the Faith, &c., All and Singular the Powers and Franchises, Privileges and authorities whatsoever and howsoever granted or to be used or exercised by the s^d Master, Wardens, and Assistants by virtue of any right, title, or interest vested in us by letters patent, custom or prescription in, for, or concerning the election, nomination, constituting, being, or appointing of any person or persons into or for the Offices of Master, Wardens, Assistants, or Clerk of the s^d Company, and likewise do surrender unto your said Majesty all our right of having or holding a Court of Assistants, and We, the said Master, Wardens, and Assistants, do hereby most humbly beseech your Majesty to accept of this our surrender, and do, with all submission to your Majesty's good pleasure, Implore your grace and favour to re-grant unto us, the said Master, Wardens, and Assistants, and our Successors, the manage and choosing of such officers who shall manage the governing parts of the said Company under such restrictions, qualifications, and reservations as your Majesty in your great wisdom shall think fit. In Witness whereof we have hereunto put our Common seal, this 23rd October, A.D. 1684, in the 31st year of Your Majesty's reign."

This course of procedure was not undertaken, however, without going to Counsel, for which advice the Company paid 10s., and also a fee of £2 14s. to Mr. Recorder for assistance in drawing the surrender and petition; the Court also determined that the document should be delivered in person, and, accordingly, the Master, Wardens, and Clerk went down to Hampton Court for the purpose, dining at Kingston on the way back, and expending altogether on coach hire, dinner, tips to clerks, etc., the sum of £7 14s. as appears by the Company's old cash book. Although this surrender of all their rights and privileges had thus been made, the affairs of the Company were still carried on as usual, and Courts were held, meetings took place, and the Company acted, generally, as if it was still in existence with all its powers intact.

Before, however, any answer was returned to their prayer, the King died, but early next year, namely, on 7th January, we read, at a meeting of the Master, Wardens, and Assistants, the New Charter was brought in by the Clerk and ordered to be opened and read, when the Company found all their former franchises, privileges, immunities, and customs pursuant to their prayer restored unto them. They then did, with all humble and hearty and loyal thanks, acknowledge his sacred Majesty's grace, favour, and goodness.

After this, the Master, Wardens, and all the Assistants then present, took the oaths under the New Charter and subscribed the Test.

The present Master, Mr. Simon Smythe, offered to the Court that as it was His Majesty's pleasure to appoint him to be Master of the Company until the next election according to the Charter, and stating that though it may be not so long as usual yet he would do all in his power to serve the Company, and concluded that as we duly and heartily returned our humble thanks for His Majesty's grace and favour to us this day, so he thought it his duty always to pray " Long live King James the Second."

This Charter, then, is the one under which the Company is now governed and guided, and amongst other features of interest bears the signature of the notorious Judge Jeffreys. A note in the minute book informs us that shortly afterwards it was thought convenient and reasonable that the remainder of the money due to Mr. Burton being £16 (he had been paid £40) for his services in procuring the said Charter, should be discharged by the Master and Wardens, which was ordered to be done accordingly.

CAP. III

Remember who commended thy yellow stockings: and wished
to see thee ever cross-gartered.

Twelfth Night.

IT is a somewhat difficult thing in these days to
ascertain with any degree of accuracy what
the art or mystery of girdle making (or girdling,
to use the old term), really consisted in; it is so long
now since the craft was a living reality, that, like
the study of a dead language, everything savours
of the past, and it is only by the most careful research, and the picking up of a fact here and there
that it is possible to get any idea of how the art
was carried on, and what the leading features
of it were; and there are also these further points
even more disconcerting, namely, that very few,
if any, genuine English girdles are to be found
at any of the London museums by which we
could get an idea of how they were formerly
made, and also that when, after long search,
the facts have been carefully sifted and are apparently accurate, later on something new crops up
unexpectedly, directly contrary to what appeared

correct before, and the whole thing has to be re-considered and done over again. The very word "mystery" is an enigma in itself, and has three or four different meanings assigned to it, all varying in their origin, and all equally probable. So far as I have been able to ascertain from the authorities, the word was first introduced in the reign of Edward III, in place of the Saxon word "guild," and it is stated that the term arose owing to the fact that the preservation of their trade secrets was a primary ordination of all the fraternities, and continued their leading law so long as they remained actual working companies. Others again say that this is not so, but that the word is derived from the French word *mestière*, craft or art. Another version traces it to the Latin word *mistera*, and there is yet another derivation from the Venetian statutes, where the word *misteri* is used for trade; so that it is a little difficult to make out what the word really does mean—but no doubt the reader will pick out the one of these four which best agrees with his fancy.

In very early times the Girdlers' Company appears to have been split up into several divisions, each of which carried out their own particular branch of the trade, and some of these distinctions remained as long as the art continued to be practised. Thus there were the Girdlers proper, who were competent to make a girdle throughout from beginning to end, and these again were split up into two great subdivisions, some engaged in the manufacture of girdles for everyday wear, whilst another and a very important branch was engaged in the manufacture of girdles and, subsequently, "bandyleers," for war service and the military, and perhaps there are more examples of these latter girdles to be seen on tombs and brasses than of the civilian. There was also a very large section of the Company who went by the name of " Brigirdlers " or " Brace girdlers," and who, apparently, were occupied in the making of an article somewhat akin to the modern braces. Others again, also a very large section, went by the name of " The Bokelers," and were engaged in the manufacture of buckles and garetters or garters, and there were also several smaller divisions which I don't propose to mention now, but will content myself with briefly referring to one or two of the more important.

As regards the articles known as "bandyleers," I think they were introduced a bit later on, as they are not mentioned in the original ordinances, and, so far as I have been able to ascertain, probably came into use with the discovery of gunpowder. They consisted of a kind of case for powder, made of wood covered with leather, and were slung with cord through the girdle, and the cover of each was made to slip up and down on the cord, so that it should not be lost. Sometimes these bandyleers were not attached to the girdle at all, but were slung from the neck upon a baudrick or border, and Fairholt says that the red or blue cord worn over the crossbelts of the Household Cavalry at the present day is a survival of the cord by which hung the priming horn or touch box. He also goes on to say that the bandyleer fell into disuse about 1670, when cartridges and patrons came in.

" Brace girdles," or " Briggirdles," imply more or less the uses they were put to, especially when we remember the old term "briggs" sometimes facetiously used for breeches and trousers; but whether they passed over the shoulder like modern braces, or were fastened in some other way, it is difficult to say.

The " Garetters," or " Garters" in the early times seem to have been almost as important as the girdle itself, judging from the particular mention of them in the ordinances, and, I suspect, were often in the nature of straps wound round the leg, as well as the ordinary strap now used as a garter. The best example I can think of is the one given at the heading of this chapter, which, it will be remembered, the unhappy Malvolio wore much against his will, complaining, later in the play, that it caused some obstruction to the blood.

At the end of the Tudor period garters were often of a very showy character, and were sometimes made of silk ornamented with spangles and other devices, and were also tied with large bows.

But the Puritans objected to all this, and they were, for the time being, cut down to reasonable limits. However, like a good deal of other gaiety, they revived again with Charles II, and in a poem written just about that time, a countryman, going to make love to his lady, thus describes his dress:

> And first Chill put on my Zunday parell
> That's lac't about the Quarters,
> With a pair of buckram Slopps,
> And a vlanting pair of Garters.
>
> *Wit Restored.*

All the various branches engaged in the working of the trade appear to have been members of the Girdlers' Company, and, as such, drew up their first set of public ordinances in the year 1344.

These ordinances were drawn up in Latin and Norman-French, and the following translation is taken from Letter Book F of the Calendar of Letter Books of the City of London:

" Be it remembered that on Saturday next after the Feast of the Translation of St. Thomas the Martyr [8th July], in the eighteenth year of the reign of King Edward III, etc., the men whose names are set forth below were sworn to keep the articles under written, touching the trade of The Girdlers, before John Hamond the Mayor and the Aldermen, read, and as befitting the common advantage, received Richard Wayte, Gilbert Broune, John Styward, William Waleys, and John Colewelle;

thereto the Mayor, Aldermen, and Chamberlain of the City of London pray the good folks, the Girdlers of the same City, that certain defaults which they find in their trade may be amended, and by certain folks of the trade be regulated, the same persons before you to be sworn to do the same.

" In the first place That no man of the trade shall work any manner of tissue of silk, or of wool, or of linen thread, if the tissue be not of such length and assize as was wont to be used heretofore, that is to say, six quarters.

" Also that no man of the trade shall garnish, or cause to be garnished, girdles or garters with any but pure metal, such as latten (or latone), or else with iron or steel.

" Also that no one of the trade shall make girdles or garters barred, unless there be a rowel beneath the bar.

" Also that no tissue of silk, or wool, or of thread, or leather, that is in breadth of sixth size fifth, third, or double size, shall be garnished unless it have a double point in the buckle and in the tongue; as also the bars with a double point down to the rowel below, that is to say, as well with reference to closheneys[1] as other (work).

" Also that no tissue or leather shall be garnished in the said trade without a rowel beneath the bar, whether it be wide or narrow.

[1] Harness.

"Also that no man of the trade shall take an apprentice unless he be free of the City, and if he be free, that he shall take no one for less than seven years.

"Also that no strange man shall be admitted to work in the trade if he will not be an apprentice in the trade, or buy his freedom.

"Also that no man of the trade shall work on Saturday or on the eve of a double Feast after None has been rung.

"Also that no man of the trade shall work in such trade at either roset or tirlet.

"Also that no man of the trade shall keep his shop open on Sundays or on Double Feasts to sell his wares. But if any strange person, passing by chance through the City upon any Feast day, shall have occasion in a hurry to buy anything touching the said trade, it shall be fully lawful for a man of the same trade, whomsoever he may be, to sell to him, within his own house, whatever he shall wish to buy, but without opening his shop.

"Also that no one of the trade shall get any woman to work other than his wedded wife or daughter.

"Also that no one of the trade shall be so daring as to work by night at the said trade on the pain hereafter written.

"Also that no man from henceforth shall make a girdle of any worse than ox leather.

63

"And hereupon it is ordained by the Mayor and Aldermen, with the assent of all the good folks of the said trade, that if anyone of the trade shall be found by the men so sworn acting against the ordinances aforesaid, or any one point of them, the first time he shall be amerced forty pence, the second time half a mark, the third time ten shillings, the fourth time one mark, and the fifth time one mark, to the use of the Chamber, and such girdles as shall be found to have been falsely made against the point aforesaid by the sworn men before mentioned, shall be burnt."

These ordinances are fairly simple to understand, and evidently were well adapted to their purpose—judging from the great length of time they lasted before any alteration was made in them. The only point which really needs any elucidation is as to the working at roset or terlit, but though I have looked up several authorities on this point, so far I have not been able to ascertain what it means, but as it was forbidden to work at either of these two particular crafts, perhaps it does not much matter.

In 1356 a writ close was sent to the Mayor and Sheriff that proclamation of the Girdlers' Ordinances should be made, and proclamation was made accordingly on Wednesday after the Feast of Decollation of St. John the Baptist (29th August).

Several other writs were issued the same year as to who might and who might not make girdles, and four Girdlers, namely, John Abraham, John Bartelot, Richard Russell, and Thomas Atte Shoppe were summoned to attend Parliament after Easter, and also four saddlers, and the matter was argued out.

These, then, were the first official ordinances, although from a study of the Letters Patent granted by Edward III in 1327, it is evident that ordinances of a much earlier date were in use and sanctioned by the Company themselves for the regulation of the trade, as indeed appears on the face of these ordinances, and probably these official ordinances were only a reiteration of, at any rate in part, those formerly enforced by the usage of the Company.

The Girdlers having got their powers were not slow to exercise them ; in fact, they seem to have used them a little too vigorously, and in the same year came into conflict with the Saddlers, who raised a great outcry and brought the matter before the King, and complained that the Girdlers were using their powers to their disadvantage, and thereupon the King issued a writ of supersedeas to the Mayor and Sheriffs directing them not to proclaim the Girdlers' patent until the matter had been argued before Parliament and some decision arrived at thereon. Evidently the Company had shown excess of zeal, because, when shortly afterwards they petitioned Parliament for powers again to exercise their right of search more than three miles beyond the limit of the City, the prayer was not granted, and yet curiously enough, under the patent of Edward III, it was enacted that the folks of the said trade who shall be chosen in the said City of London there to make search at such time as they should come into other cities, etc., might, with the folks of the same trade who were chosen so to do in the places to which they should have so come, make search, etc., and by a letter preserved in the Guildhall and dated A.D. 1354, we know that the Company actually exercised this right, the letter in question being from the Mayor, Thomas (Leggy), Aldermen and Commonalty of the City of London to the Mayor and Bailiffs of the town of Salisbury, " Notifying that John Abraham, John Bartelot, and Walter Salmon, girdlers and citizens of London, had been chosen by the good folk of the craft within the City of London to rule and survey the said craft, that it be properly preserved in all points to the common profit of the people in all cities, towns and boroughs throughout England as in the Charter of the Lord the King more plainly is contained, Desire them therefore to assist the aforesaid persons in ruling the said craft in their town, and in reforming abuses as they themselves would wish their folk to be treated in matters touching their own interest. The Lord have them in his keeping."

It looks, therefore, rather as if the Company were deprived of this right of searching in towns outside the City, as I cannot find any other example of their exercising the right, and the later charters especially confine the power to the City with a three miles' limit.

As has been mentioned, many of the guilds received their first charters about the same time as the Girdlers, and no doubt there was a certain amount of jealousy and emulation amongst them, and a danger sometimes of the craftsmen of one guild overstepping the bounds of their own particular art and trespassing on that of others, and an attempt was made in A.D. 1376 to prevent the Girdlers from working any precious metals into their girdles, and although the particular case was successful, it does not seem to have had any serious effect on the trade, judging from the numerous mentions of handsome and valuable girdles we meet with at this time. The case is as follows : a William Bonjohn, girdler, was attached to make answer to the Mayor, Aldermen, and Commonalty in a plea of trespass and deceit on plaint made by Ralph Strode, that he secretly made in his chamber a certain girdle that was harnessed with silver, whereas to make or work any plate or girdle with gold or silver is in no way belonging to the trade of the Girdlers, or to make girdles or garretters with any metal except with iron, steel, or latone, as by the ordinance of the trade of Girdlers granted at their request more fully appears.

"And being interrogated thereupon before the Mayor and Aldermen on the Thursday next before the Feast of St. Botolph the Abbot (17 June) in the 50th year, etc., he admitted that the said girdle was so made by him, and put himself upon the favour of the Court. And seeing that if the Girdlers who work with the metals aforesaid and make girdles and garretters with the said metals were to have them gilded and silvered, they might easily make as well as girdles and garretters other articles gilded or silvered and sell them for gold or silver in deceit of the people, and so it is feared might injure or deceive many persons having no knowledge of the same, it was adjudged by John Werde, Mayor, William de Haldene, the Recorder, John Chichester, and other Aldermen, and William Newport, one of the Sheriffs, that for the whole time that the said William Bonjohn should wish to keep to the trade of a Girdler and not to belong to the trade of goldsmiths, he should find sufficient surety that he would make no girdles or any other things pertaining to the trade of goldsmiths except for his own use, of any other metal than iron, steel, or latone, or any other work than such as the Girdlers of right ought to make, under the penalty of paying for the first offence 40s." No fine was inflicted, but when a few years later the same William Bonjohn was brought up again for the same sort of offence, he was adjudged to pay 40s. to the Chamber of London.

This is the only case I have been able to find, and it is clearly against the use of gold and silver in the making up of girdles by any member of the Company, except for his own use, but, as under the sumptuary laws, no one under the rank of an earl was allowed to use a golden girdle, perhaps it was not a very great hardship. I do not think, however, that the effect of the case can have been of long duration, for the reason before-mentioned, namely, the extravagance of dress at this particular time, despite the special laws enacted to prevent it, and in the later ordinances of the Company the use of gold and silver was especially sanctioned.

It will be remembered that under the Charter the use of lead, pewter, and tin in the garnishing of girdles was forbidden, and it was described as "false work," but later on this seems to have been modified by a case in 1417, when John Nasyng, Walter Colred, William Penne, and Richard Michelle, Wardens of the trade of girdlers, presented before Henry Bartone, Mayor, and the Aldermen of the City of London, three leather girdles, harnessed with tin and other false and worthless metals, as they asserted, which had been taken from William Stikeneye, dwelling on London Bridge, afterwards, namely on the 8th September in the fifth year (of Henry V) because that it was found by the Mayor and Aldermen that the girdles aforesaid were made of good leather, and durable, and that the harnessing of the same was of good and hard metal, and very advantageous for the common people, namely, of tynbasse, with but little tin intermixed, it was awarded by the same Mayor and Aldermen and assented and agreed to by the Wardens of the said trade, that the same William might in future make all such kinds of girdles and harness them with such hard and useful metal without any impediment on the part of the Wardens now, or in future to be, so that from this date the use of tin in the making-up of girdles could no longer be considered unlawful. Before proceeding any further, it will be convenient here to set out a little fully, perhaps, the powers and responsibility vested in the Company by the right of search given them by their Letters Patent of A.D. 1327. It will be remembered that there is some evidence of the Company having powers to search in all burghs, towns, etc., where the trade was carried on, accompanied by the folk of the same trade chosen to do so in that particular town, but that this right was early lost, and although petitioned for by the Company more than once, was never again granted to them.

This right of search was not peculiar to the Girdlers, but seems to have been enjoyed by them with many other fraternities and guilds from the earliest times, and when the art or craft of the guild was a living reality, was a privilege and advantage of great benefit to the Company, and sometimes also a cause of great trouble, especially when it had to be enforced, and was resisted, as was very often the case.

If we refer back to the Letters Patent, we shall see that they especially emphasize and set forth the whole method of procedure as to this right which was to be carried out by the Master and Wardens, and in former times one of the most onerous duties of the Master and Wardens was in carrying out this work, as they had to go round with certain of the freemen artizans, called the searchers and sealers, and in the words of the precept " visit all the houses, shopps, workhouses, and of all and every other person and persons free of the said Company useing or exercising the art or mystery of a girdler, and all goods which in their said searches they shall find to be bad and insufficient, or to be defectively or dreadfully wrought or made of bad, insufficient, or counterfeit matter or stuffe, to take and seize the same and every of them, and bring the same to the public hall of the said Company or Society to the end the same may be defaced or otherwise so disposed of as to the said

Master and Wardens and Assistants, or the major part of them, shall seem meet so that his Majesty's subjects may not be abused or deceived in the buying thereof, and the penalty for resistance or refusing to open any drawer, presse, or other place was £5."

The following copy of an old extract relating to this right of search will show the extreme importance attached to this duty by the various companies.

"Masters and Wardens of Cordwainers, Curriers, Girdlers, and Saddlers of London, upon pain of £40 for every year they make default, half to ye King, and the other to the presenter, shall every quarter or oftener make search for all boots, shoes, and other wares made of tanned leather within three miles of London, and seize and carry away to their Common Hall all such boots, etc. insufficiently made, curried, or wrought. None of the said Masters and Wardens shall search any persons but such as use the occupation of the said Masters and Wardens.

"The Mayor of London and the Aldermen, upon like pain of £40, shall yearly appoint 8 persons being freemen of some of the Companies of Cordwainers, Curriers, Saddlers, and Girdlers, whereof one shall be a sealer and keep a seal for sealing leather, who shall be sworn before the Mayor and Aldermen, which searchers and sealers shall search every tanned hide, skin, or leather which shall be brought as well to Leadenhall, as to any other Fair or Market within three miles of the City, and finding it sufficiently tanned or dried, shall seal the same."

The next paragraph lays down that four of the searchers and sealers shall keep one book wherein they shall enter all bargains made for leather hides or skins during the time of Fair or Market being required by the buyer or seller, and the prices taken for searching, sealing, and registering every ten hides, backs with the necks, etc., of the seller, 2*d*., and for every six dozen calves' skins and sheep skins, 2*d*., and of the buyer the same."

These searchers and sealers thus appointed had first to be presented in the following manner:

"To the Right Honourable the Lord Mayor and Court of Aldermen of the City of London. We, the Master and Wardens of the Company of Girdlers of the said City of London do hereby present unto your Worship and Worships Master Wagstaffe, a free member of the said Company, to be a searcher and sealer of leather at Leadenhall, to continue him in the said office for the year ensuing, being a person in every way fully qualified within the direction of the Act of Parliament in that way made and provided."

It will thus be seen that practically a leather girdle had to undergo two ordeals of search before it was taken by a purchaser, so that the test must have been a pretty severe one, and to show the justice and prudence observed by the Master and Wardens in their exercise of this right of search, the case of William Stikeneye given above is the only one in two hundred years I have been able to find in which the Master and Wardens were beaten, and then I cannot help thinking that technically they were in the right, but the action may have been more in the nature of a test case, as only a few years previously, viz., in A.D. 1391, the King had granted a petition of the Company, allowing girdlers to garnish girdles with white metal, and fixing the price for such girdles (which were not to be sold under one penny), and probably the Company wished to ascertain if "tynbasse" was included in the term "white metal."

It may be convenient here to say a few words about the subsidiary branches of the Company before alluded to, namely the Pinners and the Wireworkers "als plateworkers" as they are sometimes described in the minute books, although, as we have seen, the former no longer belong to the Company, being granted a corporation to themselves by King Charles I after a union with the Girdlers of about 200 years. The Pinners, as their name suggests, manufactured pins, but, apparently, not the little solid-headed wire pins we are accustomed to think of in these days, and which I believe were introduced in or about the year 1817, but something more in the nature of those now used by ladies to stick through their hats, with many different kinds of elaborate heads. These pins at one time formed an important part in every lady's wardrobe, and it is recorded that Joanna, daughter of Edward III, had no less than 12,000 of these in her trousseau, and the idea is still kept up in marriage settlements in which a clause is sometimes inserted securing pin money to the wife, and, in fact, in ancient days a very common way to get into the good graces of a lady was to present her with " pinnes," if we are to believe the writers of the Middle Ages, and " the joly clerke Absolon," in Chaucer's " Miller's Tale," in the course of his lovemaking with the carpenter's young wife, evidently knew this, as we read

He sent her pinnes methe and spiced ale.

This same young lady, too, it will be remembered, was the happy possessor of a girdle " Barred al of Silk," and this, no doubt, added to her other excellences, seems to have been too much for "that joly clerke Absolon." Unfortunately, the Companies' minute books say very little about the Pinners, and so far as they do refer to them, say nothing about the art of pinmaking, but simply mention the complaints made by the artizan pinners of the unsatisfactory state of the ordinances as regards their art, and in particular touching defects "alleadged by them in workmanshipp in

the pynnes imported into this Kingdom from forraigne parts," and as they were unable to arrive
at a satisfactory arrangement with each other,
about twenty years after the opening of our minute
books, the Pinners successfully petitioned the
King for the enlargement of their Charter, with
power to search all over England and Wales, and
ultimately were granted a Corporation to themselves, and so were quite dissevered from this
Company, and have never had anything to do with
them since.

The wireworkers, "als plateworkers," were never
dissevered from the Company, and are still nomin-
ally a branch, as the latest Charter of the Company
includes them as well as the Girdlers. They were
never so important a body as the Pinners, but
although few in number their interests were not
neglected, and in 1631, the artizan wireworkers
applied to the Court, stating that the artizans of
the Mystery were in the habit of making bad wares,
and requesting the Court to have proper rules laid
down for the protection of the craft. They were
directed to draw up such ordinances as they
considered necessary, with proper regulations for
the goverment of the art, and submit them to the
Court. This they did, and the Court sanctioned
a set of rules and arranged the necessary fines for
bad workmanship.

The art seems originally to have consisted in the

manufacturing of hooks and eyes of all sorts and sizes, and no other kind of wirework is alluded to, and I do not think the wireworkers ever formed anything much more than a very subsidiary branch of the Company, and their other title, "plateworkers," seems almost too high-sounding a name for men engaged in so homely an art as the manufacture of hooks and eyes, but it must be mentioned that it is sometimes stated how in later times the trade was developed and enlarged, and was subsequently subdivided into several distinct branches such as needlemakers, tin-plate workers, stock card and wool card makers, and lanthorn makers, and others, and directions are given as to these later developments in the trade ordinances, set out in the Appendix at the end of this book, and, although I can find no evidence of any active interest as regards these later developments in the Companies' minute books, this of course may be accounted for by the fact that it would be very difficult for the Company to exercise supervision and to control so many different trades, especially as they were always increasing in number, and gradually extended beyond the City and the three-mile limit, and it may be that the Company left all this work entirely in the hands of the wireworkers themselves, considering they had quite enough to do in supervising the art of girdling, and if this is so, naturally very little in connection with these other crafts would be recorded in the Companies' minute books.

Mention may conveniently be made here of the old shop or warehouse situated in Westchepe, in 1332, known as Girdlersselde, the property of John Potyn, a wealthy girdler of the time, who also owned eight other shops in the parish of St. Michael de Bassyeshawe, besides a good deal of other property. This selde was more in the nature of an Oriental bazaar where all articles manufactured by girdlers could be purchased, and it is quite within the bounds of possibility that before the Company had a Hall of their own, this building may have been used for their general meetings and ordinary business, but this of course is only a suggestion. This John Potyn was Master about the year 1329, and on his death left an annual quitrent of 4s., charged on this house for the maintenance of the fraternity for providing wax tapers (*fraternitatis cereorum*) before the church of St. Lawrence in Old Jewry, but whether he meant by this to indicate the Girdlers' Company I do not know, but it is quite possible that the description may have been the old religious way of describing the Company.

ARTIZANS

CAP. IV

Hie sind jr Gürtel wol gemacht
Von Läder/ artlich vnd geschlacht/
Von Rincken/ Senckel/ hübsch ergrabn/
Von Lauberck Meisterlich erhabn/
Gestempfft/ glatt/ breit vnd auch schmal/
Mannsgürtel auff das best zumal/
Mach auch stempffeyßn vnd Brenneysen/
Grab Sigel/ wie ich kan beweißn.

Der Gürtler,
Stände vnd Handwerker, Frankfurt a/M, 1568.

N O book professing to give a historical account of the Girdlers' Company could be called complete which did not set out somewhat fully the part played by the band of free brothers of the Company, known formerly (for practically they no longer exist) as the "artificers," and later on as the freeman artizans, once by far the most considerable and perhaps also the most powerful body in the Company, numbering when the trade was actively carried on, between six and seven hundred persons, divided into two great classes, the wholesale dealers and the retail, all of whom looked to the trade for their means of daily sustenance and support. Naturally the opinion of so great a body of men, all practical workmen in the art, would have great weight with the Court, more especially in matters connected with the art itself, and in fact, as we shall shortly see, their opinion, backed by their numbers, carried such authority that at times they were able to bid open defiance to and even to overrule and coerce the Court when the latter were not of the same way of thinking as themselves.

Owing to the loss of the minute books previous to the year 1622, it is impossible to say what the relations between the Court and the artizans had been in times anterior to that date, and in fact the only notice we have of the "artificers" in early times is an important public act of the Company, being a petition of the artificers of this Company joining with certain other members of Companies carrying on kindred trades to the King in Parliament complaining against foreign competition, both by the importation of goods ready made and the immigration of foreign workmen. Now that the question of alien immigration has again taken a prominent place in current events, this petition becomes somewhat interesting as showing how old the cry really is (though the class of immigrant in those days and what is complained of at present are widely different things), so that I have ventured to set the petition out somewhat fully; besides, too, the philosophy contained in it is delightful, and the language and wording in places very quaint. The petition is dated 1463, the third year of Edward IV, and runs as follows:

"Pyteously shewen & compleynen unto your wisdomes the Kynges true Liege people artificers Handcrafty men & women inhabityng & dwelling in his moost noble & famous Cite of London & in other good Cities Towns Boroughs & Vilages within this noble realme of England & Lordship of Wales howe they all in generall & everyche of them have been greteley empoveryshed & grievously hurt & hyndered by the grete multitude of dyvers Chaffares & wares perteyning to their craftes & occupations beying full wrought and redy made to the Sale as well by the handes of Straungers beying the Kynges ennemeys as other brought into this Realme of England and Lord-

81   G

ship of Wales from beyonde the see as well
by Merchauntz Straungers as Denysyns & other
persons whereof the moost part in substance is
disceyvable & nought worth in regarde to eny
mannes occupation or profite and also by the
meanes of the grete nombre & multitude of aliens
& straungers of dyvers nations being artificers
householders & dwellers in dyvers Cities Touns
Boroughs & Vilages within the said realme &
Lordship using such Handcraftes & havying &
setting awerke grete nombre of people in their
houses of their owne nations & noon other dailly
occupiyng the said handcraftes by the which the
said artificers straungers be contyneully occupied
& gretely enriched All the other artificers being
the Kynges Leiges gretely empovervyshed & not
awerke and over that grete part of the Tresores
& Richesse of the said Realme & Lordship by the
said Artificers Straungers & their Servantes is
daily conveyed & carried out of the said Realme
& Lordship into their owne Cuntries to the grete
hurt of the Kyng & empoveryshyng of the said
Realme & Lordship by cause whereof his Liege
subjects beyng artificers may not lyve by their
craftes & occupations as they might doo in dayes
passed but many of them as well householders as
journeymen servauntes & apprentices in grete
nombre at this day be unoccupied & lyve in grete
ydelnes poverte & ruyne which oftentimes causeth

hem to falle to rioth vyces and mysgovernancy &
so come to myschief & destruction to the grete
displeassure of God & grete hurt & dishonour to
all his Realme & grete rejoyssyng & comfort to
all the Kynges ennemys wheyn but yf hasty remedy
& provision be not had the said compleynauntz
be like to be utterly destroied & as whoo seyth
brought to nought in fewe daies which God de-
fend Wherefore please your wise discretions the
premises tenderly to consider & thereuppon to the
pleasure of God & eschewyng of ydelnes moder of
all vyces and mischief & in amendment of the
Common weal of this Lande to praye the Kynge
our Soverayne Lord that it please his Highnes
by the avis & assent of his Lordes Spirituel &
Temporell in this present Parlement assembled &
by the Auctorite of the same to ordeyn enact &
establisch that noo Merchaunt the Kynges born
subject Denysyn or Straunger nor eny other person
after the fest of Seint Michell the Archangell next
comyng bring sende nor conveye into this Realme
of England & Lordship of Wales eny of these
wares or thinges underwritten That is to say
(*inter alia*) eny Drepyng pannes Dyses Tenys
Balles Gloves Gurdels harneys for Gurdles of
Iron of Latone of Stele or Tyn or of alkamyn
enything wrought of eny tanned lether Cardes
for pleiyng, upon peyne to forfeit them."

The King gave a favourable ear to this petition

83

in general, only reserving the rights of several traders named in his reply, so that it is to be hoped the petitioners were soon "awerke again, eschewyng ydelnes, moder of all vyces and myschief, and so able to recover some of the Richesse of the said Realme and Lordship of Wales." The relief given, however, could only have been of a temporary nature, because it will be remembered that in Henry VIII's reign the complaints as to the number of foreigners were louder than ever, and the neglect to take any notice of this grievance coupled with the arrogant behaviour of the alien strangers led to serious riots in the City, in which many were killed.

The first mention of any importance in the minute books as to the artizans occurs in the year 1624, when an artizan by name Dickenson, with certain others, complained to the Lord Mayor and Aldermen " That there was noe execution of the ordinances of this Company touching Girdling, whereby the poore artizans were undone, and base wares made," producing some girdles before the aldermen which they said were not as they ought to be. The Lord Mayor referred the matter to the Master of the Company, who considered the matter of sufficient importance to warrant the opinion of the whole Guild being taken, and all the Company were summoned, and the minutes say "that the greatest part of the artizan Girdlers in and about London were present."

" And as touching the aspersion cast upon the

Governours and Government of this Company the Cort not only endeavouring to clear the same but also to be informed of the grievances of the artizans and of the abuses of the art if any were whereby a reformaçon may be had, did demand in the presence of all the said artizans Whether they or any of them could accuse the governors or government or any one of them in particular for not making good the statutes and ordinances as made or for not punishing offenders, Whereupon in the hearing of them all Ralph Finlay an artizan Girdler did answer that when Mr Browne was Mr he did complain against some that had transgressed the ordinances of the Company and that there was reformaçon and divers punished and that since to his knowledge there had been noe complaint. Being again demanded in a more ptçular manner whether there was not good lawes made and such as will meete with the abuses of these times the answere of them all was that the Lawes in being were good and such as would meete with the abuses of the present times. Being alsoe again demanded whether the statutes and ordinances of the Company were not duly put into execuçon they answered that they were and that there was noe fault in the Governors and Robert Rearwan artizan Girdler did acknowledge in the hearing of them all that the Governors had been more readie to redresse abuses than they had bin to complain."

From the above it will be seen that, at any rate, the artizans were well satisfied with the administration of the Company's ordinances at the time when our minute books commence ; but four years later, namely, in the year 1627, a petition was presented to the Court by several poore persons as well freemen of this Company as of other Companies using the art of guilding of buckles, which seems to have had very considerable effect, and was, in fact, the inauguration of a lengthy struggle between the Court and the main body of freemen artizans, which lasted many years with varying success on either side, and was only terminated by the grant of a new charter and an entirely new set of ordinances drawn up and approved both by the Court and artizans.

The petition in question informed the Court " that Girdles and Hangers trimmed with copper harness had been refused for his Majesty's service as being unserviceable as the same were for the most part slight and dreadfully made. The metal also being very brittle and not so serviceable as harness made of iron this being contrary to the ancient custom of the Company."

On receipt of this petition the Court at once took prompt action, and it was ordered that notice be given to all freemen, by the Beadle, that after the Feast day of our Lord God, now coming on, no girdle or hanger should be trimmed with copper harness the M^r to seize all goods so made and the offender to forfeit and pay such fine as the ordinances of the Company allowed. The Court also caused patterns of several sorts of harnesses to be brought into the hall and there viewed by divers artizan Girdlers, who adjudged the same as being very fit patterns to be followed, both for strength and workmanship, and a further order was made that they should be set forth as samples, both by the M^r and Wardens on the next election day to be held for the Yeomanry of the Company, and that if any person or persons should hereafter make any harness or girdles which should be of other strength or workmanship, then they should forfeit such sums as by the ancient Fellowship of the Company should be thought fit.

This order was enforced with very great strictness, and at once caused friction, and although the minutes show that this fining was most impartially carried out, no one being spared, not even a member of the Court itself, as the following proves: " Roger Haydon, one of the assistants, was fined 1s. 6d. for making 36 children's girdles of bad materials. The girdles were ordered to be defaced and the stuff given back to him." Nay, the Court must have been made of leather itself to judge from the following curious entry : " Two bundles of unmade girdles were taken from widows Maybury and Bliss, 'young widows,' they were ordered to pay 5s. each by way of fine for making and selling unlawful wares." Still, next year (1628), the M^r and Wardens informed the Court that they had been called before the Lord Mayor on the petition of several members of the Company who had been fined for bad work, and who had appealed against the justice of such penalty, but that on the cases being heard the members were adjudged to be in the wrong and ordered to pay their fines.

Although the Court had thus won their case, evidently they did not feel very sure of their ground, for almost immediately afterwards, on the complaint of an artizan Girdler accusing the Court of not putting the ordinances into execution, more especially the ordinances touching those who "set on worke such as had not served 7 years at the art, and also for setting foreigners and maids on worke," the following minute occurs " Inasmuch as the ancient ordinances of the Company do not give sufficient power to the Cort to punish the artizans for bad work and insufficient workmanship and other abuses of the trade, it was resolved that the M^r and Wardens call on several of the artizan freemen to advise and confer with them in devising such ordinances as were necessary, and make new rules and regulations so that they may be submitted to the Lord Chief Justice for approval, so that the Company may have power to punish such offences for the good of His Majesty's subjects," but before anything was done the whole Company was summoned again, and it was found that infringements had taken place and also that several other offences had been committed contrary to some recent ordinances established by the Court, but inasmuch as the new ordinances had not been confirmed and passed by the Lord Keeper of the Great Seal,[1] the Court decided that they could not punish the offenders, but they determined to call together certain of the artizans to assist them in framing a new set of ordinances to be passed and confirmed "in order that the Governors might have full lawfull power to reforme the abuses of these times and punish the offenders for the good of his Majesty's subjects."

Next year two of the artizans, by name Walter Dickens and Philip Jenkins, were summoned before the Court for tynning of garnish for girdles and using turned harness contrary to the ordinances of the Company, "and on being remonstrated with behaved in a very contemptuous manner." They were fined forty shillings, but refused to pay, and as they persisted in their refusal, after six months endeavouring to bring them to reason, proceedings were taken to enforce the penalty. On

[1] This was necessary under an Act of Henry VII. These new ordinances most probably were made a few years before the date of our first minute book.

this Philip Jenkins seems to have submitted, but Walter Dickens still persisted, and once again the Court was successful on appealing to the Lord Mayor, and he had to appear before the Court and apologize, and "did promise to conform himself for the future and demean himself properly," whereupon the Court ordered his fine to be returned to him, for which, according to the minutes, "he was most thankful." Shortly after this the artizans presented to the Court "a petition of grievances," complaining, amongst other things, "that many Girdlers did exceed in taking of apprentices above their number, that many Girdlers set on worke forreyners, women, and maids, that the trade was used by some that never served 7 years," and there were also several other complaints, and lastly they complained that the M^r and Wardens never of recent years called any of the artizans to go round with them in their searches, and they asked leave to be allowed to search of their own authority.

The Court answered the complaints in the same order as they were set out, and as to the question of search reminded the artizans "that they had constantly called on members of that body to accompany them on their searches, and would again on occasion, but as to giving libertie unto them to search by themselves, the Cort neither holds it fitt or convenient." This answer did not please the artizan Girdlers, and in November of the same year they presented another petition of grievances of much the same tenor as the last, and the Court answered that the charges made in it were too vague and general, but as to the right of assisting the M^r and Wardens on their searches, if they would present six able persons of their number the M^r and Wardens would pick out two to accompany them on their rounds.

Notwithstanding that the Court had thus given way on the matter of searching, their troubles were by no means over, as next year (1633) the artizans appealed to the King, alleging " that anciently the Companie did consist of a M^r, Wardens, and yeomanry, out of which yeomanry officers were heretofore chosen, with power to search and redresse abuses hindering the said trade and to put in execuçon the aɛts and ordinances made for the good thereof whereby they thrived, and the commonwealth was then well served and that of late divers merchants, silkmen, and other trades being come into the Company, and bearing the chiefe offices thereof had put downe the yeomanry and appropriated to themselves the sole government of the Company, and being men of other trades had neglected the suppression and the reforming of abuses."

Evidently the artizans, annoyed by the refusal of the Court to accede to the demands in their last petition, and knowing by experience it was

no use appealing to the Lord Mayor, had determined to appeal to Cæsar himself.

The King referred the matter to Mr. Attorney-
General, and forty of the artizans attended at his
chambers in Lincoln's Inn Fields with counsel, the
Master and Wardens also appeared by counsel,
and " whilst denying the authority of the Court of
Laws to interfere in the matter, expressed their
willingness to meet these grievances by allowing
the artizans to draw up their own regulations for
the management of the trade, and submit the same
to the Court for approval, and if these received
the sanction of the Court the Master and Wardens
were willing to carry them out."

Meantime, whilst the Company were quarrelling
amongst themselves, the trade was slipping from
their hands, as a great number of foreign girdles
made of French and also Spanish leather, and
known as Caddis girdles, began to be imported into
the country and were openly sold in the City, and
the Master and Wardens took counsel's opinion as
to whether they would be safe in seizing them, but
counsel gave it as his opinion that they would not,
so nothing could be done; furthermore, everyone
began to manufacture girdles of an inferior quality
and finished with brass instead of iron buckles,
which latter practice was only stopped by the
strong hand of a royal proclamation headed from
Whitehall, which runs as follows:

"Proclamation prohibiting the making up of Belts, hangers, and other wares for men's wearing for war service with brass buckles, such buckles had been ordinarily made of iron by a Company of buckle forgers, buckle filers and trimmers and dressers of buckles, members of the Society of Girdlers, London. These persons and their families were likely to be impoverished by the use of buckles cast in brass, which were brittle and not so serviceable as those in iron." The use of brass buckles was therefore forbidden. To digress here for a moment, it is very marked how brass has ever been ranked by the artizans of the Girdlers' Company as a false and worthless metal for the garnishing and harnessing of girdles, and in the earlier times it seems to have been looked upon almost in the light of a crime to use any of it in the making up of a girdle. Chaucer even appears to notice this, and when describing the dress of the Canterbury Pilgrims makes special reference to the fact that their knives and girdles were not trimmed with brass :

An Haberdasher and a Carpenter
A Webbe a Deyer and a Tapiser
Were alle yclothed in o liverie
Of a solemnpne and grete fraternitie
Ful freshe and new hir gere ypiked was
Hir knives were ychaped not with bras
But all with silver wrought ful clene and wel
Hir girdles and hir pouches every del.

Meantime the dispute between the Court and artizans went on, neither party being willing to give way sufficiently to make a compromise possible, but after four debates before Mr. Attorney-General the latter drew up a long report to the King, signed by both sides, which report practically admitted the right of the artizans to have six of their number attend the Master and Wardens on their searches, and that all wares seized for bad workmanship should be carried to the hall and there "viewed and tryed" by these six and the Court, and it was especially stipulated that at least eight of the Court who "viewed and tryed" must belong to the trade of Girdlers.

Immediately after this the Master caused all Girdlers free of the Company "to assemble and meete together to advise upon some course to be taken about the making of good wares." " But by reason of the great multitude and incivility of some who would permit none to speak but themselves, nor approve of any other course or reason than what they themselves intended and produced," nothing could be settled at that meeting except that a joint committee of the Court and artizans was appointed.

This committee met several times, but the demands put forward on behalf of the artizans were so drastic and unreasonable, practically putting the whole Company into their power, that the Court was unable to agree to them, and ultimately each side appointed a counsel and the matter was again referred to Mr. Attorney-General, who, probably rather weary of the quarrel, ordered a general meeting of the Company, in which each side was to be represented by counsel, "to try and see if their present differences might be decided." Before the general meeting was called, however, the matter was thoroughly threshed out by the joint committee, and after several meetings of this body agreement was reached, and a set of ordinances drawn up, but on the summoning of the whole Company to approve them, "many of the artizans refused to set their hands to them," but instead drew up on their own initiative thirteen propositions and submitted them to the Court, who answered them all, but as some of the replies did not please the artizans nothing was done.

It would be wearisome to go through the numerous meetings of the next two or three years because, although many propositions were put forward and argued by counsel for their respective sides, nothing was ever definitely settled, and the feeling at times ran so high that the two counsel themselves seem to have become involved in it, and on more than one occasion accused each other with some bitterness and warmth, but after carefully reading through the reports of all the meetings, which are very conscientiously entered by the clerk of that time, and some of them at great length, I have come to the conclusion that the artizans did not really want a settlement, and the truth of the matter was they seem to have made up their minds that the Court was composed of men not really belonging to the trade (as was, in fact, the case as regards some of them), and so, not in real sympathy with the Company, all sorts of annoyances were practised, and the Court were constantly being called before the Lord Mayor and Court of Aldermen, either on the ground that the usages of the Company were being enforced in an arbitrary manner, or not enforced at all. They were even called before " The Starre Chamber," and "contemptous carriage and uncivill speech" seems to have become a frequent and favourite relaxation on the part of the artizans; these means, however, did not have the desired effect, so that the artizans again petitioned the King, and this time he was asked to take the power out of the hands of the Court and vest it in the hands of the artizans. The King naturally followed the usual course, and again referred the matter to Mr. Attorney-General, and meetings both at his chambers and at the hall again took place in which each side was represented by counsel, who argued the matter both before Mr. Attorney-General and the Court. At length, in 1635, a settlement was reached, and the Master presented the agreed terms between the Court and the artizans to Mr. Attorney-General, who ordered that a new charter should be prepared and the ordinances renewed on the agreed lines, but, owing to a fresh quarrel that broke out this time among the artizans themselves on a dispute between the wholesale and retail body, the matter was once more postponed. Two years later, however, the wholesale and retail dealers seem to have come to a satisfactory arrangement, and in 1637 the Master, Mr. Edward Taylor, who had once been clerk, again called all the Company together at the request of the artizans themselves, who stated they desired a treaty of peace, and thus addressed them : " That before Christmas last he caused certain ordinances to be read, which by divers able artizans of this Company were held fitt to be confirmed for the good of the art and artists, and some other things in the Company, and having then taken great care to draw things to a head to settle peace in the Company, yett at that time some of the artizans then present caused great disturbance, but now, being upon a treaty of peace, he put them in mind of the Company's motto, 'Love as Bretheren and continue as Friends,' which, though it was of few words, yet was very significant, and desired them carefully to observe the same and suite themselves that the meanest member might not rent or dissever himself from the body or head." After which he further told them that if they thought meet the proposed ordinances should be read unto them again, where-upon Leonard Hickford, one of the said artizans, made answer, " That they should have a new charter for the government of their trade accord-ing to their desire, and they would doe nothing untill then." To which the Master, on behalf of the Court, replied, "that they conceived they had thought of peace but find it otherwise, and withall told them that they could not expect more in reason than what the Company had already con-sented unto, which he did now recapitulate." The artizans, upon hearing the proposed terms read out, asked for copies to take away, but the Court replied, " that if they would meete in the Hall they should have them read unto them; so long as they would noe body should disturbe them, but to have them to carry about from place to place out of the hall they should not, soe they depted nothing being concluded on."

Shortly afterwards, however, the effect of this meeting was seen in the artizans presenting to the Court the draft of a new Charter, restoring to the artizans their ancient privilege of presenting cer-tain of their number to the Master and Wardens, who picked out from these those whom they con-sidered fit to accompany them on their searches, with certain other conditions framed much on the same lines as those formerly settled by the re-spective counsel on either side. This Charter, after one or two meetings, was agreed upon, after the Court had struck out a clause giving the artizans power to vote in the election of Master and Wardens, which, if passed, would have practically put the power of the Court into their hands, as the artizans outnumbered the Livery by about ten to one; the Court, however, insisted that the election of the Master and Wardens should remain with the Livery "as it hath been tyme out of minde," and the artizans had to give way on this.

This Charter, being properly engrossed, was presented to His Majesty, the petition starting with a declaration "that they had now att last accorded amongst themselves ye differences that for a long tyme had been between the members of their incorporation."

His Majesty referred the matter to Mr. Solicitor-General, and after one more adjournment the Charter was granted according to the petition, and, although curiously enough no mention appears in the minute books of the final order, or the date of its promulgation, still, as the Company has now got the Charter in its possession, we know that it was actually granted, and, as has been mentioned in a previous chapter, the date was 1640, so that the struggle had practically lasted for over twelve years, and, as is somewhat pathetically set forth in another minute, the struggle had "put the Company to great charges." Even then, apparently, not all the artizans were pleased, and it is evident that it did not give general satisfaction all round, as the same year we find an artizan girdler summoned before the Court for saying " that he would break the Charter of this Company, and that the same was of none effect, and that if this Company stood out with him he would overthrowe their Charter, and when charged with the said opprobrious words he could not well deny the same, and did acknowledge himself sorrowful for his said rash and inconsiderate speech, and promised never to doe the like, and prayed the Court to pass by this affront, which the Court did after admonition for his rash and inconsiderate speech."

We also find in the same year that the artizans presented certain of their number to the Court, who picked out sixteen of these called the Yeomanry, and these latter assisted the Master and Wardens in what must have been an onerous job, in viewing the girdles provided and prepared "for his M^{atles} warre service and intended speedily to be carried into the Tower." Matters between the Court and artizans gradually cooled down after this new Charter, and a more friendly disposition grew up between them, so that a few years afterwards we find a joint committee appointed, who drew up a new set of ordinances in reference both to the actual working of the art and also the government of the Company, and these ordinances (which are the present ones under which the Company acts) it is especially recited are made in pursuance of a statute of King Henry VII of famous memory, whereby it was enacted that "noe Master, Wardens, and Fellowshipps of crafts and mysteries should take upon them to make any acts or ordinances in diminution of the prerogative of the King, nor of any other, nor against the common profitt of the people without the same being examined and approved by the Chancellor or Threasurer of England, or Chiefe Justice of either bench." It so happened that these ordinances received the consent of all three, being ratified and confirmed by the Earl of Rockingham, the then Lord High Chancellor, Sir Francis Pemberton, the Lord Chief Justice of the King's Bench, and Sir Francis North, Lord Chief Justice of the Common Pleas.

It is not proposed to set out these ordinances here, as if so the matter in itself would make up quite a small book, and much of it, too, especially the regulations referring to the art or mystery of the guilds, as the Wireworkers, otherwise Plateworkers, were included as well as the Girdlers, is no longer of such essential importance as to warrant the recital, but it will be sufficient to mention here that they were practically agreed upon many years before they were actually passed and promulgated, "but inasmuch as the funds of the Company were very low on account of divers great sums borrowed upon the seal of the Company," there was no money to get them approved and passed by the Lord Chancellor, and the matter remained in abeyance for some years, and then the Fire of London occurring, the Company suffered so heavily that the matter was again delayed for some years more, so that it was not until the year 1682 that they were seriously pushed forward and considered, and received the sanction of the Crown, and then curiously enough, just after they were passed, the girdle began to drop out of fashion, so that the ordinances in relation to the art itself cannot be said to have stood any serious test, as when the trade began to decline naturally, of course, did the number of artizans, and from a body of between six and seven hundred strong they gradually withered and withered away, getting of less and less importance, until at this present day the expression artizan Girdler is an unknown term, and for many years past has not been heard in Girdlers' Hall.

CAP. V

Warden of men and with so many cares.
Homer.

WE have now considered the origin of the various charters, and the ordinances as to the "artizans" or "hand craftymen" of the Girdlers' Company, and the next matter that claims our attention is the Constitution, and to understand this properly it will be necessary to look into and examine the ordinances from another point of view, namely, the aspect of the executive and governing side. The Girdlers' Company at the present day consists of a Master, three Wardens, called respectively Upper, Middle, and Renter Warden, a Court of Assistants, Livery Freemen, and Apprentices, and in addition there are the two stewards chosen annually from members of the Livery, and also the executive officers, such as the Clerk, Surveyor, Beadle, and Porter, and formerly, as has been shown, there were the Yeomanry Searchers, called sometimes Warden Substitutes and the Whifflers, but the last-named body practically lost its usefulness, and ceased to exist at the same time as the artizans.

And first as to the Master. He, of course, during his year of office, is head of the Company, and, like the King, can do no wrong; his title goes as far back as the reign of Edward III, before that time the Master being known as the Alderman of the Guild, and it will be remembered that in a previous chapter reference was made to the first head of the Company of whom we have any knowledge, viz., in 1180, and his name is given as Ralph de la Barre, and he was called Alderman of the Guild.

The greatest respect is always shown to the Master; he is " The Worshipful Master," and so he is generally styled on all state occasions, or when addressed in his official capacity, and this custom of addressing a man in authority as " Worshipful " is mentioned in books as far back as " The High History of the Holy Graal," so that the custom is sanctioned by immemorial custom. Everybody gives way to the Master, and his expression of opinion and wishes are always received with becoming deference and consideration by the other members of the Company, and in former times anyone who was at all inclined to forget the respect due to his high office stood in some danger, as constantly appears from the minutes, and to show disrespect to the Master was not only considered to be an insult to him, but also an affront to the whole Company. Thus we read, in A.D. 1625, " Whereas Symon Jefferson had misbehaved himself to the Master and one of the Wardens of the Company, not only in unseemly carriage, but also in opprobrious words, whereby he not only lay an affront upon them but also upon the whole Company and the government thereof, for which offence being summoned before the Lord Mair and found culpable he was committed to prison," but on his signifying his willingness to make an apology, a regular submission was drawn up (of which document he had to pay the costs) setting out all the facts and stating : " And Whereas it pleased the s^d Mr Lee (the Master) and others of the said Company to move the Lord Mair to remit my said imprisonment upon my promise of submission, whereupon His Lord^{sp} ordered that I should repaire to the next Court of Assistants to be holden for the said Companie, and there acknowledge my fault and submit myself to the censure of the s^d Cort, I doe therefore in accomplishment of the s^d order acknowledge my said fault, and am very sorry for my said offence and doe humbly intreate the Cort to be pleased to passe by the same, and doe willingly submit myself to the censure of the said Cort touching my said offence In Witness whereof I have hereunto subscribed my name the 29th day of Aprill, 1625.

Whereupon it pleased the s^d Cort in hopes of his conformity and better carriage for the future to passe by his offence and not to inflict any fine upon him for the same." Sometimes, however, the Court was not so lenient, but insisted on the payment of a "fyne" as well as the costs of a release.

The Master is chosen by election, which takes place in August and must be on or about the feast day of the Company's patron saint, St. Lawrence, and the mode of election is very quaint, being done by whisper to the Renter Warden, the latter going round to every member of the Court and Livery assembled in a General Court and asking them their choice; but the proposed Master must have two qualifications. According to the ordinances he must have held or fyned for the office of Upper Warden, and he must also be "a discreet, able, and fitt person," and the latter qualification will sometimes carry him straight to the chair without filling or fining for the office of Upper Warden, as will shortly appear.

As soon as "the choyce" of a Master has been made, the Wardens are elected, being proposed and seconded in the ordinary way; they all make a declaration in which, among other things, they promise justly and indifferently to execute or cause to be executed their various offices. They are then clothed in the proper robes pertaining to their offices, take their seats, and in the evening are crowned, and are thus constituted officers for the ensuing year.

Now that the trade of girdle-making has died out of England the offices of Master and Wardens, although they still carry with them a certain amount of work and responsibility, are not, of course, nearly so onerous as in former times, when the Master and Wardens had constantly to go round and examine into the workmanship of all those who followed the trade of girdle-making, and, in fact, were engaged in the work of general inspection for the Company, and this duty was of so exacting a character that it is not surprising that nearly every year we find a struggle on the part of those on whom "the choyce" fell to escape office, and all sorts of excuses and devices were put forward, the favourite one being the old plea of illness, so that although, in 1620, Mr. Geoffery Eyre, on his election to the office of Renter Warden, wrote and asked to be excused as he "Lay very sick and more like by ye judgment of man to dye than lyve," yet for many years afterwards we find his name in the books of the Company.

Some idea of the work involved on those who held the various offices in former days may be gathered when it is remembered that in one search alone the Master and Wardens are recorded to have seized and brought to the hall as many as 133 dozen girdles, which, upon examination, were found to be defective, and in 1640, " The M^r and Wardens did declare that of late they were un-reasonably troubled about searching makers caring not to what trouble and expense of tyme they put them unto sending for them almost every day in the week," so that it cannot be wondered at that men every year were content to pay a fine rather than serve any of these offices, and these fines, too, were sometimes very heavy, a Mr. Gumill, in 1626, paying 100 crowns for the excusal of the three warden's offices, whilst one Richard An-drewes paid as much as £200 to be excused all the offices, and by this means became the founder of one of the Company's charities, as will be more fully set out later on; on the other hand, the fine was not always payable in hard cash, as in 1625 a Mr. Davis had been excused serving the office of Renter Warden conditionally on his finding a brace of bucks for the use of the Company whenever he might be called upon for them, and yet another instance a few years later on, " Mr. Richard Ellis did intimate in recompence of the Companies Love toward him in exempting him from serving the office of M^r of this Company, whereunto they had lovingly and feelingly chosen him at Election Day last, he had sent into the Hall (which he freely gave the Company) 5 Corsletts, 4 Musketts, and 4 headpieces which were lovingly and kindly accepted by the Court"; but the hardest case I think was that of Henry Scarborough, who, in 1669, petitioned the Court to be excused serving the office of Master, pleading as excuse "indisposition of body as well as the distance of his habitation, he living over 100 miles from the city." This being taken into serious debate, it was resolved that he be excused upon payment of a fine of £40. This he consented to do, and thanked the Court for their kindness. Considering the difficulty of travelling in those times this certainly seems a heavy penalty. The Court, however, were not always contented to let people off serving the offices on payment of a fine, and in 1742 two members having for several years past refused to serve any of the offices, were removed from the Court of Assistants, and a few years later a member of the Court hit upon the idea of serving all the offices, including that of Master, by proxy. This he did, but the Court at the conclusion sent him an account of the fines payable for not serving the various offices, and he had to pay.

Under the present ordinances the fine for not serving the office of Master is £20, and the same for the Wardens.

Another interesting point about the office of Master is shown by the following minute: "24 June 1667. At this Court according to ancient custom the Wardens for this Company for the year ensuing are usually nominated, and it happening that John Cudworth was standing next in Course on the Livery Rolls for the place of Renter Warden This Court was informed that the said John Cudworth had lately paid his fine to the Chamber of London for Alderman and Sheriff of this City It was resolved that he should not be put in nomination for the said place of Renter Warden, but that according to the custom of this Company he should be put in nomination on the next election day for the Master of this Company which was done and he was chosen Master."

The Master's lot has not always been a happy one, nor has his reign invariably been for the whole term; thus, in 1687, Edward Nourse tasted the sweets of office for a few weeks only, being elected and chosen Master, but almost immediately removed from office by order of the King, who issued a command to that effect.

This order came from the Lord Mayor and Court of Aldermen, and runs as follows:

" 25th September 1687. By the King's most Excellent Majesty and the Lords of His Majesty's most Honourable Privy Council.

"Whereas by the late Charter granted to the several Companies of London It is provided that his Majesty His Heirs and Successors may by Order of Council from time to time displace or remove the Master Wardens and Assistants of the several Companies or any of them and thereupon the place or places of such person or persons shall be void And Whereas His Majesty hath thought fit that several members of the said several Companies should be removed His Majesty in Council is pleased to order and it is hereby ordered accordingly that the following members be removed and displaced from being Master Wardens or Assistants of the said Company, and his Majesty is further pleased to order that the Lord Mayor and Court of Aldermen do forthwith signify His Majesty's pleasure herein to the said Company." Accordingly the Master, two Wardens, and eleven Assistants were removed from the Company's list.

Later on in the same year seven more members of the Court were removed in the same manner.

Afterwards, however, many of them were restored to the Court of Assistants by order of the King by his Royal Letter, and Mr. Nourse subsequently fulfilled the office of Master. On one or two occasions, as in 1721, the Master has died during his year of office, when the senior past Master, usually called the Father of the Company, has been elected to the office for the remainder of the year, or an entirely new Master has been elected. It is unnecessary to set out here the duties the Master has to perform in these present times, but it is enough to say that they vary from presiding at the Court down to donning an apron and cutting up the broken meats for the almsfolk after the Livery dinner.

At the end of his year of office it is usual to pass a vote of thanks to the outgoing Master, but the following minute will show it is not a matter of course: " 11 Sept., 1788. At this Court the conduct of Mr. Haigh Master of the Company for the year past was taken into consideration, when it was unanimously resolved that the following animadversion on him should be entered on the minutes of the Company, to wit, The unexampled inattention to and neglect of the duties of the first officer of this Company for the past year instead of calling for the usual compliments of the General Court to a past Master, produced a murmur of discontent strongly declarative of their disapprobation of the conduct of Mr. G. F. Haigh as Master of the Company, a memorial of which is accordingly entered on these minutes in order to hand to future officers a proper caution against incurring the same disgrace."[1] At the expiration

[1] Within the last few years the Master has been decorated with a badge of silver gilt representing the Company's arms worked in enamel and silver which he wears hung round his neck on all occasions when he is acting in his official capacity as Master. This badge was presented by Judge Philbrick on the termination of his year of office in 1880, and still more recently Mr. Morrison Fairclough, another past Master, has presented smaller badges of the same character as the Master's for the use of the three Wardens, and these badges are all worn round

of his year of office the Master joins the ranks of the past Masters, "most potent, grave, and reverend seigneurs," who are sometimes called upon, and are all eligible to be chosen Master again, and the senior of these is, as above mentioned, usually the Father of the Company, or, as he was formerly styled, "the Ancient Member," and generally takes the chair in the absence of the Master, and further there are always two or three past Masters on the Committee to assist the Master and Wardens with their advice and experience in the Company's affairs.

Among the names of Masters of the Girdlers' Company who in former times held high civic offices, or added distinction and dignity to the position, are the following: Benet le Seinturer, who was Sheriff of London A.D. 1216, John de Prestone, mayor, 1334, Sir Stephen Soames, Lord Mayor in 1598. The latter, however, was not very popular with the Company, judging from the following: " It was ordered and agreed forasmuch as he had altogether neglected the Company, and had not left any remembrance as a testimony of his love, and to declare to posterity that the Company had such a member, that his arms set in the window of the Hall should be taken down, and in place thereof the arms of Mr. Richard Chambers,

their necks attached to collars of blue and gold, the Company's colours.

who is now the ancient member of the Company, be set up." Three years later another Girdler Master, by name Henry Anderson, was made Sheriff of London. In 1634, the Master dying in office, Robert Bell, one of the first Directors of the East India Company, and a famous city merchant, was chosen Master, and at the end of his year of office gave the magic carpet about which we shall speak later on. It is constantly stated that Thomas Sutton, the founder of Charterhouse, was a member of this Company, but I am afraid, after very careful search, there is no actual proof in support of this; if he was, I do not think he took a very active interest in the affairs of the Guild, certainly we are not mentioned in his will, although he does not seem to have forgotten any body or institution he had any connection with. The statement, I think, must be founded on the fact that at this time (1620 *circa*) there was a Thomas Sutton a member of the Company, and his name is always cropping up because he was a carpenter, and had a good deal to do with the repairs to the Hall, and somebody, seeing the name, must have jumped to the conclusion that he was the famous Thomas Sutton.

During the last fifty years or so the Girdlers' Company have had many Masters who by their position, and the way they have carried out the duties, have added dignity and distinction to the office, but as they or their descendants are happily still living, it would be invidious to set out their names and distinctions here.

Of the three wardens the duties of the Renter Warden, as may be supposed, have always been, and still are, the most onerous, as he is practically the treasurer of the Company, and accordingly is required to enter into a bond, with two sureties, to deliver up all plate and goods of the Company that may come to his hands without fraud, covin,[1] or delay. Only once in the whole of its history has the Company had to enforce this bond, and that was in 1771, when the Renter Warden was expelled the Court, and it was ordered that the bond be put in suit against him and his sureties, but as it transpired that he was in prison in Dunkirk, it was ordered that nothing more be done in the matter. However, in 1776, the Renter Warden in question appeared before the Court again, and asked for his livery and steward's fine to be returned, and the Court gave him the latter after deducting the amount due on his account. The office of Renter Warden was another post formerly much shirked by those who were chosen on account of the amount of work entailed, as in addition to assisting the Master and other wardens in their searches, the Renter Warden formerly also

---

[1] The reader no doubt will remember that the word " cove " is still used in certain circles of society.

received all the rents and other moneys coming to the Company, and the memory of this is still retained by the fact that the accounts for each year are called the accounts of the Renter Warden who happens to be in office for that year, and all rents and receipts of the Company are signed by the clerk twice, once for himself and once as agent for the Renter Warden, so that here again we find nearly every year those who were elected pleading their inability to serve the office, and submitting to pay a fine for not doing so, and many and various were the excuses put forward to try and avoid serving. It remained, however, for a member, by name John Jones, to test the truth of the old proverb that ignorance is bliss, for when chosen for the office he pleaded that " he could neither read nor write," and as this was perfectly true the Court was obliged to pass him over; however they fined him £15 for not serving, "which was cheerfully and lovingly paid."

The Court of Assistants derived from the Saxon Council of thirteen, as was previously stated, is nominated, elected, and chosen by the Court from the members of the Livery, and in accordance with the ordinances are to form the Common Council of the Society and to continue during their lives, although there is a power of removal which in ancient times appears to have been pretty frequently exercised, and once, namely in 1685, as mentioned before, members were removed wholesale by order of the King and Privy Council, and at the same time nineteen members of the Livery were removed from the Rolls of the Company; four of the former, however, were subsequently restored, and it was not often that the Company suffered from outside interference.

All Liverymen are liable to serve on the Court, but they must be of seven years' standing, unless some special cause be shown to the contrary. In these times, of course, the chief business of the Court is the management of the Company's own affairs and their charities, but in former days, when the trade was a living reality and the members of the Company all lived round about the hall, the Company was carried on in a much more clannish and patriarchal manner than at present, and the powers of the Court were not only exercised in respect to judging as to the fitness of the wares seized in the four quarterly searches, but extended to the private affairs of the members of the Company to an extraordinary degree, and they took cognizance of matters that in these times would be considered quite outside their sphere of influence. Thus we find in 1642 that one of the assistants "did complain against Jonadab Edwards for opprobrious and scandalous words in Edwards' shop in saying that he, naming Mr. Wildney, was a 'cheater,' and that he would justify the same."

Mr. Edwards appeared before the Court and stated that he only called Mr. Wildney "a Juggler." The Court ordered him to pay a fine of 5s. 8d. to the poor of the Company.

Another entry, a bit earlier, namely in 1622, shows that the Court had almost magisterial powers of settling disputes amongst members. "Mr. Warden Street complained of Wm. Taylor (his late servant and a free brother of the Company) that he owed him £10 19s. 7d." The latter was ordered to pay 19s. 7d. at once, and to bind himself to pay the remaining £10 within six months, and again in 1745 a member of the Court having given a note of hand for £10 to another member of the Company was struck off the Court of Assistants for not meeting it. Members of the Company were not allowed to go to law with one another without the sanction of the Court, and many instances occur as to this. Thus, 24 Jan., 1624. "Alsoe at this Court, George Gilbert, a poore free Brother of this Company complained against Andrew Raven, Pynner, a free brother alsoe of this Company, touching a certain debt owing by the said Raven to the said Gilbert, whereupon it was ordered that Mr. Arthur Lee, Mr of this Company, should when it pleased him to appoint a day to hear the difference and decide it, and that if the said Raven should refuse to perform what the Mr should order, that the said Gilbert should have liberty to take his case of lawe against the said Raven for his said debt."

In private quarrels, too, the Court exercised their discretion, as the following example out of many shows (1633), Richard Gyles and Bernard Shepperd, free brothers of the Company, who complained of each other's ill language. After consideration it was ordered that "they should be friends and forgett and forgive what had formerly past between them, and that each party should seale for libel a generall release to the other of all matters controversial or debates whatsoever."

According to the ordinances the Court shall come and sit in their gowns and other decent apparel, and the penalty for appearing without their gowns was 2s. 8d., and also the same penalty was enforced for having their gowns faced with satin instead of silk or stuff. No meeting of the Court can take place unless the Master and Wardens, or any two of them, and eight assistants are present, and as great difficulty was found in always getting sufficient numbers to attend, notwithstanding the fact that the fine of 1s. 8d. was constantly enforced for non-attendance, and also the punishment of expulsion, it was ordered in 1733 that the first twelve, or so many that shall come to the Hall before eleven o'clock at their next meeting for business, shall receive thirty shillings to be divided equally amongst them, notice being given thereof at the bottom of their summons, and that a watch shall be set by the clerk by Guildhall clock, which shall determine the time.

The members of the Company living so near it is no surprising thing to find the Court summoned so early as eight o'clock in the morning, who attended to business until dinner-time, one o'clock, and then dined, and an order was made that if possible all business was to be finished before dinner.

The ordinance for keeping order and decency in ye Court of Assistants enacts that but one person shall speak at a time to the matter then in debate, and shall address the Master, and that every member speak in his turn according to his seniority, and that all debates be serious and without any reflections, reviling speeches, or expressions that may justly give offence to the said Court or any officer or member thereof, and that no one reveal the secret debate of the Court sub poena 40s.

The next consideration is the Stewards, who are chosen annually by the Court, and who formerly were responsible for four of the yearly feasts at "their owne equall charge," the sum of £8 2s. 8d. being paid to assist them out of money left by Mr. Lawrence Robiant in 1558, and also by Mr. Cuthbert Beeston in 1680, for that purpose, and they had " to make, find, and provide the like dishes of meate, drinke, wyne and other provision usually accustomed," and to prevent any mistake as to the quality and quantity of the dinner to be provided, the Court thoughtfully ordered that the clerk should serve each of the stewards personally with a copy of the usual and accustomed bill of fare.

Innumerable instances occur in the minute books of the endeavours made to try and escape this office of steward, which in reality could have been no light duty, as in addition to the bequest of Mr. Robiant and Mr. Beeston, the office of steward usually cost each of the participants quite £30 for the four yearly feasts, so that it was in reality a very heavy tax on a man, and those selected were generally very ready to pay that sum rather than serve the office, and the pleas put forward for non-serving vary from the ordinary excuse, such as that of Christopher Maynard, who asked to be excused because, as he piously put it, "it had pleased God to afflict his family with sickness," to the bold defiance of two stewards, who, being recommended to submit themselves to the pleasure of the Court, refused to do so, and threatened to drag the matter before the Lord Mayor, which so exasperated the Court that they replied in the same strain and ordered them to provide a dinner by a certain day, or in default to be summoned before the Lord Mayor, which threat ultim-

ately had the desired effect, and the stewards
submitted. But the greatest struggle the Court
had was with a Mr. William Clifford, who seems
to have accepted the office, but declined to provide
the dinner, and the clerk reported that he had served
Mr. Clifford with notice of the Company's inten-
tion to compel him either to serve or pay the fine
for the office of steward by a certain day, also
with a copy of the necessary and accustomed bill
of fare, and the minute goes on to say that on
being served with the above Mr. Clifford treated
the matter very contemptuously, but that in the
forenoon of the day named he had sent his attorney
to represent that he was very low in circumstances,
and had attended himself before the Court with
his apothecary to plead his indisposition of health,
and that he was unable to discharge the office of
steward, whereupon the Court, after stating that
they were unwilling to distress anybody, instructed
the clerk to draw up an affidavit, which Mr. Clifford
offered to swear, that when he had paid all his just
debts he was not worth £120, and he attended before the Lord Mayor and took the oath accordingly.
Sometimes, though, the Court had a more grateful
task, as the following shows, " Whereas Joseph
Tilden, one of ye liverie of this Companie, was on
the xvii day of August last, being the election
day, chosen steward of the four quarter dynners
for ye livery of this Company, and was att a Court

of Assistants houlden for this Companie the xxiiii of September last, uppon his earneste intreatie freed from executing of ye said office on paying ye somme of £xxx by way of fyne to the use of this Companie. Now forasmuch as ye said Joseph Tilden in obedience of ye said order did very lovingly on this day make payment of ye said £xxx It was thoughte meete and so ordered for ye better encouragement of ye said Joseph Tilden in the continuance of his good and orderly carriage in the Company to restore unto him fyve poundes, part of the said £xxx, which was done accordingly, and by him very thankfully accepted."

Subsequently the Court adopted a general practice of exempting Liverymen from serving the office of steward who were willing to make an affidavit that when all their just debts had been discharged they were not worth more than £100.

January 25th, 1667. After consideration of the great loss sustained by the Company by the late dreadful fire being taken into serious debate, it was proposed that for reason that the Company had no stock in money, and considering the great difficulty this Company would have for months in carrying on the affairs of the Company and making provision for the rebuilding of their Hall and other considerations, that whereas the stewards of the four quarterly dinners for the Livery of this Company did yearly and usually expend £30 apiece and upwards at their two feasts, and whereas also the fine for every person that did not hold the said place was set by an order of the Court at £30 apiece, ordered that the future stewards pay a fine of £25 to the Company to help towards the Company's rebuilding their hall and parlour, and it was further ordered that all public feasts usually offered by this Company shall for the space of five years be wholly suspended and forborne.

In these days, of course, the stewards no longer provide the dinner, but fine for the office instead, but this fine is still mitigated by the amount of money left for that purpose by Mr. Robiant in 1558 and Mr. Cuthbert Beeston in 1680, and the Court further endeavours to alleviate the harshness of the office by asking for the pleasure of their company at the various meetings during their year of service.

In considering as to the Livery, it must be borne in mind that this body now forms the largest number of members of the Company, and are its very life-blood, although in former days, when the trade was actively pursued, this remark, as we have seen before, would not have been true, as the freemen artizans were in number a long way ahead of all the other branches of the Company combined. Thus, in 1666, the Court[1] and Livery between them numbered eighty-one, whilst the freemen artizans

[1] Strictly speaking the Court are also of the Livery.

numbered 690, and as each freeman was entitled to have two apprentices bound to him, and also to "set on werke his wedded wife and daughter," it will give some idea of what an extensive trade "Girdling" in the City of London formerly was.

Regulations are laid down for "the choyce" of the Livery, and the Court have the power "to call elleƈt and admitt into the Livery or Cloathing of the said Society such person or persons free of the said Society as they shall think fitt meet and able and such persons shall accept and hold on the Livery of the said Society and pay the usuall fyne for the use of the Company."

It will be observed that this power is very strong, amounting, in faƈt, to compulsion, and many are the instances of the persons so called delaying "to accept and hold on the said Livery, and pay such fyne as aforesaid."

The following is the ancient form of notice sent to the freeman calling on him to take up his livery:

"Whereas the Master and Wardens of the Art or Mystery of Girdlers London by and with the assent of the Court of Assistants held at their hall the 24th day of March last did eleƈt you on their Livery or Cloathing of the said Society as a fitt meet and able person to be of the said Livery and Cloathing Now you are hereby requested (as you tender your oath) and the good and welfare of the said Society personally to be and appear at a Court of Assistants to be held for the said Society at their hall Basinghall St London on Thursday the 21st day of April at 10 of the clock in the forenoon then and there to accept and hold on the Livery of the said Society and pay to the Master and Wardens or Keepers of the Art or Mystery of Girdlers London for the use of the said Company the usual fyne of ten pounds of lawful money of Great Britain as hath been accustomed and if you shall refuse or neglect or delay to accept and hold the said Livery and to pay such fyne as aforesaid you will forfeit to the said Master and Wardens or Keepers of the Art or Mystery of Girdlers London the sum of three pounds six shillings and eight pence to be on default of payment thereof recovered or levyed in such manner as by the orders acts and ordinances of the said Society are appointed.

"Dated 22nd March, 1600.

"To THOMAS GOODFELLOW.

"N.B.—If you attend pursuant to their summons your fyne will be mitigated to Five pounds.

"Signed, DANIEL HEATHFIELD, Beadle."

These summonses seem to have been issued wholesale, judging from entries in the minute books such as the following: "12 June, 1626, Ordered that the Beadle summon the 29 Freemen whose names were selected to take the cloathing of the Company." And two years later there is another minute to the same effect: " The Companies stock being low and impoverished by reason of the heavy calls of money for the King, twenty-one yeomen were summoned to take up the Cloathing of the Company." Sometimes the Court had great trouble to enforce their summonses, and an obstinate freeman might delay coming to hold on to the Livery for years, as the following minute, dated 27th May, 1632, proves: "Whereas a Freeman by name Isley had been chosen on the Cloathing 1626 and after accepting the same had refused to pay his fine of £10 and after having had much trouble the Court had been compelled to complain of him to the Lord Mair who had committed him to prison for the same contempt and whereas he was afterwards chosen in August 1627 to be one of the Stewards and the Court being then unable to bring him to reason had again to appeal to the Lord Mair who thereupon committed him to the Goal of Newgate until he promised to submit himself to the Company and conform to their orders and to pay the sum of £25 (which had been assessed on him) Nevertheless still persisting in his contemptuous carriage after giving bonds for the £25 refusing to pay the same After endeavouring for six years to bring him to better behaviour the Court determined to put him off the Roll of the Livery, and ordered that in future he be summoned to attend the meeting of the yeomanry."

In the year 1656, at the Court held in April, no less than fifty-five freemen were ordered to be summoned to take up their livery, and the Court imposed a fine of £3 6s. 8d. on all those who failed to attend the summons, and there are many instances in the minute books of the infliction of this fine for the contempt of members to the summons.

There was an ancient custom of the Company for every member on his being admitted to the freedom to give a spoon, and this was kept up until 1747, when it was enacted that in future the 10s. paid by persons made free of this Company be entered distinctly and apart, i.e., 3s. 4d. for their freedom and 6s. 8d. as a gift to the Company in lieu of a spoon, according to the ancient usage and custom of the Company. Accordingly we find soon afterwards in the same year the following: "Mary Temple made free by Patrimony, she gave 3s. 4d. for Freedom, 6s. 8d. in lieu of a spoon, 2s. 6d. for Poor Box, and 2s. for stamps." This entry is also remarkable as being one of the earliest entries showing stamp duty payable, and also of a woman made free, although the custom of women taking up their freedom in the Girdlers' Company was a very common one.

Sometimes the freedom and Livery could be

obtained by bargain, especially when the Company's funds were low, as the following entry in 1680 seems to show: " Mr. Woodman, one of the assistants, informed the Court that he had a friend inclined to take up his Freedom and Livery in the Company, but that he would not give more than £10." The Court expressed themselves as willing to treat with him thereon. And again there were times when the Company were so hard pressed for money, especially during the Revolution, that we even find an entry such as this: "The numbers of the Livery having decreased the Court, considering the difficulty of advancing and increasing the same, ordered that the sum of one guinea be paid to the Hall Keeper at the Guildhall for every person he brings to accept the freedom of the Company." And in 1760 the state of the Company was so parlous as, owing to the lack of freemen from the utter decay of the trade, the Company almost went out of existence altogether (the modern revival of these ancient guilds had not then begun); so much so, in fact, that Mr. Walsh, an old Master, observed that the Livery list of the Company was so greatly reduced in number that it was very difficult to find persons to fill the various offices of the Company, and being concerned lest the same should fall into decay for want of proper members to support it, he offered the following proposal for the consideration of the Court, namely, "That an order be made authorizing any member of the Court to invite and encourage persons of credit, reputation, and fortune to become Free Members and Liverymen of the Company by offering the Freedom and Livery of the same to their friends and acquaintances, without paying any fyne or being at any expense for the same (stamps and the fees payable to the Clerk, Beadle and Porter on these occasions only excepted)." The Court, considering this matter to be of too much importance to be settled at a small Court, deferred the question until the next meeting, and although curiously there is no entry on the minutes showing that the matter was again discussed, shortly afterwards a Mr. Kite was admitted to the Livery without paying the usual fine, but only the before-mentioned fees and stamp.

This expedient was not adopted for very long; fortunately it was not necessary, and the Company has since then varied the fine for admittance half-a-dozen times, until the last few years it has remained more or less stationary, or at any rate not on the downward grade. The Livery, down to about 1750, all wore gowns, and it was customary for the Beadle to carry cloth to all such as were chosen of the Livery, but this custom, like a good many others, has long since passed away, but the memory of it is still kept up on the election of a liveryman, when, after he has made the declaration to be true to the King's Majesty, to obey the Master and Wardens, and to keep secret all the lawful counsels of the said fellowship, the Master of the said Society, according to the ordinances, shall cause the Beadle to put a livery gown upon him, and the said Master after the usual manner shall put a party-coloured hood upon his shoulder, after which the said Master and Wardens, each in their order, shall give to such person his and their hands, saying the usual and accustomed words of admittance. This is still done, and the new liveryman is then formally taken round by the Beadle, the latter also wearing his gown and carrying his staff, and introduced to all the members of the Court by name, each of whom in turn rises in his place from the Court table and shakes hands with him; later on, if there is a dinner that night, the Master invites him to dine, when, as it is his first night of joining the Guild, he has the honour of sitting at the top table with the other guests of the Company.

Before leaving the discussion as to the Livery mention must be made of what was known as translating a member, that is, transferring a freeman or liveryman from the guild he happened to belong to over to the guild which had the control of his art. This was always a somewhat difficult matter, as the guilds were very jealous of losing their members, and very good cause had to be shown before the mother Company would part with their petitioning brother, however anxious he might be to leave them and go over to his new guild, and to expedite matters sometimes a gift of silver or a piece of plate was mentioned as likely to be presented when the consent was obtained, as in 1662, when one Horsman, a free brother of the Company, having become a brewer in South-wark and the Brewers' Company importuning him to be translated from this Company to their own. Upon debate held upon the matter Horsman attended and expressed his great regret at leaving the Company and promising to bestow a piece of plate of the value of £5. Whereupon the Court ordered that upon his sending to the Renter Warden, for the use of the Company, a piece of plate (the value to be left to his own discretion) he shall be translated.

In the reign of Charles I the Girdlers' Company, with about a dozen other of the Guilds, petitioned the Lord Mayor and the Aldermen, his brethren, against this translating of members, at least in large numbers, the petition setting out that on information of the Company of Brewers the Council have written to the Lord Mayor and Aldermen to take order that the brethren of all other Companies using the art of brewing should be translated into the Company of Brewers. They set forth reason why this would be very inadvisable, and

pray the persons addressed to give such information to the Court that this dangerous innovation
may not proceed.

As regards apprentices, the Company has the
usual power to admit and bind apprentices to their
respective members, and to make free such as
have served their apprenticeship. The ordinances
enact that " Noe master should take an apprentice
unless born of English parents or naturalized, and
that noe man should have more than two apprentices at one time," and the breach of the latter rule
was a fruitful source of complaint, and one which
appears several times every year in the minute
books, and if proved, the master was always made
to surrender any he had over the two allowed, and
by way of punishment was fined. For some reason
or other it was formerly the custom in England
to complain of the harshness of mothers-in-law, and
this rather ill-mannered jape lingers sometimes
even to this present day. Richard Northy, however, a freeman of the Company, who was accused
in 1635 of keeping more than the just number of
apprentices, had evidently found the case otherwise, as may be gathered from his reply to the
accusation. " Whereunto the said Richard Northy
made answer that he had in noe way infringed the
said orders, for the apprentice whereof the s^d Mr.
Carpenter complained was not any that was taken
or bound by him, but was left unto him by express

words in the will of his deceased mother-in-law, wh^{ch} will, wth the probate thereof, he now produced in Court," and the Court was obliged to allow his claim.

An apprentice, of course, was a very valuable asset, and the Company were very strict in enforcing the rule as to numbers, although sometimes they had great difficulty in doing so, and in 1623 it was ordered "that the Lord Mair should be made acquainted with the disobedient and uncivil carriage of John Apthorpe, who, being ordered to put away an apprentice by him taken contrary to the ordinances of this Company, did not only detaine him, but used very irreverent speeches at the Court, to the end his Lordship might inflict some corporal punishment upon the said Apthorpe for his said contempt to the deterring of others."

Formerly the number of lads apprenticed was considerable, sometimes as many as fifty being bound in one year. No apprentice could be bound for less than seven years, and it was no uncommon thing for the term to be as much as nine. On being bound, they had to be presented at a Court of Wardens, and pay a fee of 2s. 6d., but owing to the fact that the Lord Mayor and Aldermen had the custody of orphans under age and unmarried of deceased freemen of the City, by an act passed in the reign of William and Mary, it was enacted that every apprentice should pay 2s. 6d. when he was bound to the fund for orphans, so that the Company after this lost the fee, and had to pay it into the Chamberlain's office in support of the orphan tax. In addition to being presented at a Court of Wardens, the apprentice had to be enrolled in the Chamber of the Guildhall of the City of London, and before the Chamberlain, and this had to be done within the first year of his apprenticeship. The Company were constantly called upon to admit some poor boy as an apprentice to one of their members at the request of some great man, and in particular the Lord Mayor and Court of Aldermen on many occasions caused poor Bridewell boys to be thus bound to the trade, and on these occasions not even the traditional 2s. 6d. was payable.

Girdler apprentices seem to have been just as troublesome as any others, and there are two notes of letters written in Latin as early as 1354, preserved in the Guildhall, from Thomas Leggy, Mayor to the Mayor and Bailiffs of Oxford, for the recovery of a runaway, by name Stephen, son of Roger Woderove of "Wyderyngset" (Withernsea), in the county of Norfolk, apprentice to Peter de Pary, girdler, and there are other letters also about the same date in reference to Girdler apprentices, which can be seen in the calendar of letters from the Mayor and Corporation of the City of London.

The Court is empowered, if necessary, to punish apprentices for any breach of the covenants in their indenture, and there is an instance in the minute book of 1622 where one Edward Holt, having married within the seven years of his binding, was disfranchised of all the benefits of his servitude.

If the apprentices were sometimes troublesome, it must be admitted that the masters were not always reasonable, and in some cases the Court interfered when, in their opinion, the conduct of the master was over-harsh. Thus, in 1635, when Richard Watt, an apprentice, sent a petition to the Court alleging that "he had endured weeks of woefull captivity in the white lyon prison in Southwerke upon the pursuit of his master, Andrew Raven, who further showed inhuman carriage toward him in binding of him naked to a wheele, and in beating of him, so bound, with a jackrope, and all to force him to confess matters he knew not of, thereby to accuse one of his fellowes." The Court took the petition into consideration, inquiry was made, and ultimately he was liberated at the instance of the Court.

Sometimes, when the Court was unable to bring about an agreement between master and apprentice, they caused the latter to be turned over to another master, and so saved him his years of service and prevented him from losing his start in life; thus in 1622, "Whereas Wm Cowley, the apprentice of Thomas Drayton, had complayned to the M^r of this Company that his said Master putt him from his service, not giving him anything for to doe, the said T. Drayton appearing at this Court, and both parties being heard att large, it appeared that the offence for which the s^d T. Drayton had so putt away his said apprentice was for that he had brought into his said Master's house a lewde person, that had taken from thence a silver bowl, but for that it appeared to this Court by all circumstances that the said apprentice was mostly deluded by the said person and was not anyway privie to the said fact, and for that the said T. Drayton could not accuse his said apprentice of any notorious crime or allege any materiall matters against him, and for that the said apprentice was willing and offered to make restitution of the said cupp so soone as it should please God to enable him to doe it, it was ordered that the said apprentice should submit himself to his said Master, and upon his said submission his said Master should receive him again into his service, and although the said T. Drayton was at first very unwilling, at length he was contented to accept of him again." Next Court, however, the said T. Drayton again brought the matter up, and desired to be relieved of his apprentice, and, as he persisted, the Court eventually turned the boy over to another member of the Company. There is a mixture of simple piety and disregard of immorality about this entry that is particularly refreshing, and one cannot help wondering if a modern court in a like case would consider that "nothing materiall was alleged against him." When the apprentice had served his term, he attended at the Hall, "and was made free by apprenticeshipp by the appearance of his Indenture and the testimony of his said master."

It may be fitting here to say a few more words about the freeman artizans and their powers. It appears from the minute books that it was customary for them to meet annually at the hall on the feast day of St. Michael the Archangel, and choose twenty of their number and present them to the Court, who selected sixteen of these, called the Yeomanry, and these Yeomanry appointed four of their number, whose duty it was to attend the Master and Wardens on their search for bad work, and they were known as the Warden substitutes; this has all been spoken of before in a previous chapter, but it may as well be pointed out that the reason such great discrimination was used in selecting these four searchers was because the opportunities for bribery and tyranny were so great, that it was of the utmost importance to choose honest and upright men.

The Warden substitutes also collected the quarterage from all freemen not being of the Livery, and the money so collected was distributed with the consent of the majority of the Yeomanry in the concerns of the art and the relief of the poor.

In 1687, to encourage a larger and better attendance of the Yeomanry, it was ordered that at the next meeting 40s. be expended in bread, cheese and beer for their refreshment, and after that date the following item appears annually in the cash book:

" For Cakes, Cheese, Bread, and a Barrell of Stronge Beere for a refecion for the Yeomanry of this Company, £3 10s. 6d."

One other body of men, who now no longer exist, must be referred to in passing, namely, the Ushers, or, as they were quaintly termed, the Whiflers or Whifflers. These also were selected annually out of the main body of the freemen by the Master and Wardens, and it was their duty to attend upon the Court and Livery as Whifflers, and to perform all such services as might be appointed by the Master and Wardens, and any freeman chosen refusing the office was liable to a penalty of 20s.

These also were fed once a year, namely, on Lord Mayor's day, and dined with the other servants of the Company at a cost not exceeding £4.

The officials of the Girdlers' Company are the Clerk, Surveyor, Beadle and Porter, and they are chosen by the General Court, and, with the exception of the Surveyor, in accordance with the ordinances, are elected for one year only, or until the choice of others for Master and Wardens.

In former times the Clerk resided at the Hall, and this proved a somewhat fortunate thing at the time of the Fire of London, as the Company at that time was served by rather an able clerk, by name Richard Davies, and although of course he could not save the hall, it appears from the minute books that he managed to carry off safely to his country house "at Hoggesdown," a fair amount of the Company's treasures, such as their Charters, documents of title, books, and plate, and in the next year, 1667, "the Master and Wardens brought before the notice of the Court the loss and expenses sustained by the clerk of this Company in consequence of the late dreadful fire, in moving the stocks and goods of the Company to his country house, and they now thought fitt, and ordered accordingly, that the sum of £30 should be allowed and paid to Mr. Davies towards the said expense by the Renter Warden out of the first money that came to hand."

In this country clerks are very often looked upon as particularly sober and quiet sort of people, but apparently some of the clerks of the Gilders' Company were an exception to this rule, and one of them seems to have followed the lead of a former Lord Chancellor of England, and to have been addicted to dancing, as the following minute shows: "There having been many complaints concerning the balls having been so frequent for many years, and there being several complaints from various persons of the disturbances caused thereby by quarrels happening at the door amongst coachmen and linkmen at the gate, after several debates it was ordered that there should be no more Balls held, excepting the two allowed annually to Mr. Hayting, the tenant of the Ladies' parlour, the clerk to be allowed the sum of £6 in lieu thereof.'

On one occasion the clerk seems to have filled the office of Renter Warden, and he employed a deputy to do the clerk's work; however, he did not hold the two offices long, and resigned the position of clerk "as he knew that some of the Court thought that he ought not to hold the office."

In 1627 the reversion to the clerkship was granted to William, clerk-servant to Edward Taylor, the then clerk. This caused a serious difference of opinion in the Court, " but after two debates and two divisions, it was carried in his favour for one year, and so on from thenceforth at the will and pleasure of the Company, according to his demerit." At subsequent Courts efforts were again made to upset this, but the order remained, and whereas before that time the clerks were not subject to annual re-election, ever since then they have only been elected for one year, or until the appointment of others for Master and Wardens, and this is now so according to the ordinances.

The Company has not always been fortunate in its selection of clerk, as the following entry in 1743 shows: " The Court, considering the great inconvenience they have laboured under, in carrying on the affairs of the Company at this and their last meetings, from the clerk's not attending, together with his great neglect in not entering the minutes carefully, his neglect in not summoning several members of the Livery (though often reminded of the same by several members of the Company), to the great prejudice of the Society, and this Court finding it impracticable to transact the business of the Company with such a clerk (though they have for some years past tenderly admonished him of his duty), do therefore, by the unanimous consent of this present Court, request and desire the Master to order the Livery to be summoned on Thursday, 5th May next, in order to suspend the present clerk, and to proceed to the choice of a new one, for properly carrying on the business of the Company, which this Court with great reluctance finds has been totally neglected."

The ill effects caused by this clerk's negligence remain to this day, and on more than one occasion the writer, when asked to look up some name of an old Girdler, whose descendants allege belonged to the Company at that time, and who are anxious to trace him, has been compelled to acknowledge that no mention of his name occurs in any of the

Company's books, and in addition to this the minutes of that time and the cash books were kept in an extraordinary slipshod fashion, the most important resolutions and orders of the Court being entirely omitted, and their purport only to be arrived at from what subsequently transpires.

Accordingly the Livery were summoned, and a new clerk chosen, who turned out rather worse than the former one, being especially weak in his ideas of *meum* and *tuum*, and the Company sustained a small pecuniary loss through him. So it was ordered in the future that the Clerk should give a bond, or find security, and that is still the rule.

The Clerk transacts the general affairs of the Company in accordance with tradition and custom, and the wishes of the Master and Court for the time being; he also keeps the minutes, and if he neglects to read them at a meeting of the Court, under an old by-law of the Company he was liable to a fine of 4*d.*, to be paid to the Company.

At the end of the eighteenth century, the Clerk's salary was £20 a year, with a fee of 13*s.* 4*d.* for the yeomanry, the same fee curiously enough "for washinge ye napery for the year," and a further fee of £1 " for engrossing the grand accompt." In addition he was given a residence at the hall for himself and family, if he had any, with a special allowance for coals and candles, pens, ink, and

paper. He was also entitled to several perquisites
of wine, and the Stewards were ordered to prepare special dishes for him and his family, all of
whom dined in the Hall on the occasion of the
four yearly feasts. As was inevitable, these things
all tended to get abused, and in 1815 the Court
abolished all this, and the Clerk was given a fixed
salary in lieu of all perquisites; he was still allowed
residence at the hall, which was continued until
quite recent times, and he was further continued
in the charity salaries, and still receives various
sums, varying down to one of 4d. per annum, left
for the clerk by different pious benefactors.

Clerks have become past Masters, and past
Masters have become clerks, and the late clerk, Mr.
G. E. Philbrick, could claim the latter distinction,
whilst in or about 1637 Edward Taylor, who had
formerly been clerk, but had tendered his resigna-
tion, became Master of the Company.

The important office of Surveyor to the Company is not referred to in the ordinances, and the
first mention of it I have come across is in 1681,
when the sum of £12 12s. was ordered to be paid
to Mr. Emmett the Surveyor for his assistance
in the designing of the Hall, and for seeing to the
scantlings being built in all respects according to
the articles.

The ancient office of Beadle to this Company
was formerly often filled by one of the alms-

men, but this was abolished in the middle of the eighteenth century, the last almsman to fill the office being a man of the somewhat quaint name of " Offspring Brown"; whilst the next Beadle was a past Master, one John Symonds, and in consideration of the position he had held in the Company, the Court excused his wearing his beadle's gown, excepting on election and other general days of the meeting of the Company.

In ancient times the Beadle's office was looked upon as entailing almost as much responsibility as the Clerk's, and his salary was £12 a year, with various fees, but for many years previous to the Fire of London, the following item occurs in the cash books, in reference to the Beadle's salary: " To him more as a gratuity by order of Court in respect of his weakness of Bodye and great charge of children and extraordinary paines in the Company's Business £14," so that he drew £26 a year, besides his perquisites, until the Fire of London, when the Company were so hard hit that he had to support " his weakness of Bodye and his great charge of children," without any salary at all, as the Company had no funds to pay him. However, they compensated him in another way, as he happened to be a tenant of one of the Company's houses, and the lease fell in shortly after 1666, and the Court granted him a long lease of the premises without imposing the customary fine, it being clearly understood on both sides that this favour was granted in lieu of his drawing a salary, and in addition to this he was also " put on to the clothing " without paying any of the usual charges. The Clerk, too, at the same time, appears to have carried out his duties without any salary, but as he seems to have been a well-to-do man, and even able to lend the Company money to assist them in their temporary difficulties, it was not so important in his case. In 1663 the Company purchased a very handsome silver-topped staff for the Beadle, at a cost of £7 1s. 6d. This staff, which has engraven thereon the Company's arms, is carried before the Master and Wardens on certain state occasions, among which may be mentioned the annual visit to church. At the same time a lesser staff, also " tipt with silver," was purchased for the use of the Porter at a cost of 13s. 9d., and this also forms part of the Company's "formalities " on state occasions. Formerly the beadle, and also the porter, had perqusites of wine, but this was all abolished more than 100 years ago.

An ancient office that has quite died out, but which deserves a passing reference, is that of "the Company's carver," who formerly attended at the hall, on the days of the four yearly feasts, to cut up the joints, and the remuneration for his services was a fee of £1 a year.

CAP. VI

ENTERTAINMENTS

He can live without love—-what is passion but pining?—
But where is the man who can live without dining?
Meredith.

THE old time popular imagination that City Companies existed merely to spend their time and funds on Gargantuan feasts of Syracusan prodigality has long ago given way to ideas more in accordance with the true facts of the case, and it can be safely affirmed that in these days the public no longer estimate the worth of an alderman by his weight; but although, of course, the number and character of these functions have altered very much since the days when Hogarth depicted a City feast, still, the City Companies even now occasionally foregather in their halls for the purpose of a good dinner, and rightly so, too, as without these periodical gatherings and meetings, which tend so much to promote good-fellowship amongst the various members of the Guild, it is not too much to say that formerly the very existence of some of the Companies might have been imperilled, or at any rate, their usefulness seriously impaired, as naturally, men would not undertake the responsibility and trouble of administering their trusts and supervising the various arts and crafts without some recompense for their pains, and even at the present time it cannot justly be said the festivities are superfluous, as at probably no gatherings do men of so many different social standings and views meet together to exchange ideas, and so help to get a better knowledge and appreciation of each other and their various views and ideals, and another point to be borne in mind is that the Companies do not spend their money in a selfish and exclusive manner only amongst themselves, but the open-hearted hospitality and generosity of the City Companies is of worldwide notoriety.

The Girdlers' Company too, are not more backward in this part of their duty than in any other, and one of the privileges most highly prized by members of the Court is the right of occasionally bringing a friend to dine at the Company's hall, which privilege is undoubtedly very old, although it is impossible to say when it was first exercised, as a perusal of the oldest minutes the Company possess shows that it was clearly an ancient custom even at that date, and although there have been times in the history of the Company when the privilege has had to be curtailed and sometimes even abandoned from lack of funds, still the Company have always revived it when better days dawned, so that in reality the custom can never be said to have died out, but only to have been in abeyance for the time being.

The earliest record I have been able to find of a Girdlers' dinner is in 1422, but that was not at Girdlers' Hall (being just before the original hall of the Company was built), but the meeting took place at Brewers' Hall, and I believe that the books of that Company show a record of this with the amount of money the Girdlers paid for the use of their hall.

To come down to the times of our own minute books there are many entries in connection with this question of dining and entertainments generally, but before considering them in detail it is important to remember the changed conditions under which the Company is carried on ; in those days the great majority of Girdlers lived within a few hundred yards of the hall, and as the trade was then a living reality and the means of their gaining their daily livelihood, the hall, of course, was the great centre for the gathering of the clan, and a place where they were accustomed to drop into all day and every day on some matter or other, either, perhaps, to inspect the sample girdles kept as standards of workmanship, or perhaps to arrange a trade bargain with a brother Girdler, or to discuss the affairs of the Company or the City with another brother Girdler or even sister (for it was a very common thing for women to be made free in those days), and also the Court dispensed justice there and decided on the private quarrels amongst the members of the Company. Their children, too, played in the garden, then a much larger place than now, according to Faithorne's map of London, published in 1658, just shortly before the hall was burnt down, and this also appears to have been the case after the Fire, as John Ogilby's map of London, published in 1677, makes the Company's garden appear to be slightly over fifty yards in length and about thirty-three yards broad. The children, too, were taught dancing in the ladies' parlour, and religious services were also held there, the room being lent free on condition that any member of the Company might attend who pleased, so that it will be very easily seen that at the time we are considering the hall was a very prominent feature in the lives of most members of the Company, and another, and this perhaps the most important point of all to be remembered, is the part played by the ladies of the Company, who in those early days attended the four yearly feasts as a matter of course, and also the ball held on the day of the election of the Master and Wardens. The hall was also used for breakfast parties, balls, and suppers, and lastly, when a good Girdler died, he was buried from the hall, the Company marching with his body to the church, so that it will be readily understood that the Girdlers' Company formerly bore a much more clannish and patri-archal character than at present, and the affairs of the different members were much more mixed up together and their lives interwoven with one another than could possibly be the case under present conditions.

Perhaps it would not be uninteresting to con-sider a little more fully the mode of life in those days for Girdlers. To begin with, meetings of the Court were much more frequent than at pre-sent, and during some period of the year were held as often as every fortnight, and if business was very brisk even more frequently. No dinner was held after all these meetings, as the Court met so early, namely, at eight o'clock in the morning, and in compliance with the ordinances arrayed in their gowns, those coming without them or not having them faced with silk being fined two shil-lings and eightpence each. Sometimes they break-fasted at the hall, and in the old Renter Wardens' accounts such items as the following are common : " Payd for wine, beer, bread, and cheese, for breakfast the sum of 16 shillings and ix pence." After that they set to work until one o'clock, the dinner hour, and by an order of the Court work was, if possible, to be finished before that hour. If the day happened to be one of the four yearly feast days the ladies then arrived, and here, unfortunately, trouble sometimes arose, owing to a decided preference on the part of some of the past Masters' wives for sitting at the top table, and this was the cause of many disputes, not only amongst the ladies, but even at the Court itself, and the matter was not finally settled until 1698, when the Court hit upon the plan of having them called by name, and it was ordered " for the future, to prevent further disputes, that the ladies should be called and placed in manner following : The Master's wife, the wives of the Wardens next her in their several places in the inside of the table moving from the lower end upwards, and the old Masters' wives next them in the inside, the Master and Wardens' friends on the outside, and then the old Masters as many as can sit there."

This being satisfactorily arranged, the next thing was the bill of fare, as it was called, and a perusal of the following one, a copy of the identical bill served on Mr. Clifford, the recalcitrant steward, will show it was as English as its name :

BILL OF FARE

6 dishes of Fish consisting of Trout, Turbot,
and Soles

Lobster and Shrimp Sauce

16 Chickens (8 roast and 8 boiled), four in a dish,
making in all four dishes of Chickens

4 dishes of Cauliflowers, Cabbages, and young
Carrots
2 Westmorland hams, one to a dish
2 Venison pastys, one chump of beef
2 Haunches of Venison, 1 neck of Vension with
French beans
Jelly and gravy
2 Marrow Puddings, 4 Codling tarts creamed
8 dishes of Fruit
1 Leg of mutton and Greens
8 dozen of port, 2 dozen of Madeira, 1 dozen
Lisbon, 1 dozen Mountano.
Bread, Beer, and Cheese as usual.
For the clerk:
Two Dishes of Trout and Soles, with Lobster and
Shrimp Sauce, 1 dish of Chickens.
Bacon and Greens.
The above particulars to be very good.

In addition to this the Company always added
something out of the house stock "for the amendment of the Feast," and on this occasion a very
favourite dish was provided, namely, "two Keggs
of Sturgeon."

This quantity was provided for sixty-four people,
and I cannot help thinking that it must have been
after dining at one of these feasts the witty French-
man remarked "that Englishmen take their pleasures sadly." But, perhaps, the amount was not so
excessive as it seems at first sight, owing to the

laxity of rule that prevailed, many of the members bringing their sons and also servants, all of whom of course wanted to be fed, and who quarrelled amongst themselves over the food in various parts of the hall, so that the dinner must have savoured somewhat of a rough and tumble style, and what with the struggles of the ladies for precedence, and the scramblings of the men for food, could hardly have been very enjoyable, at any rate according to our modern notions. At last the Court had to take notice of this, and in 1682 it was ordered, that "considering the disorder occasioned by the younger Liverymen bringing so many of their servants to the dinners, it was ordered that hereafter no person of the Livery below an Assistant should presume to bring either his son or his servant, for that by experience it hath been observed that the said servants have greatly disparaged the said feasts by taking off dishes before it was proper from the Livery Tables, and dining themselves at the same time in the said room, which is very indecent and improper at such public dinners."

By another order of the Court every man had a bottle of wine set in front of him at the beginning of the feast, and, as they started the dinner with port, the thirst at the end must have been something agonizing. During dinner the following toasts were honoured:

" Esquires and Gentlemen all, the Master and Wardens drink to

" 1st. Church and King.

" 2nd. The Prince and Princess of Wales, and the rest of the Royal Family.

" 3rd. Prosperity to the City of London and the trades thereof.

" 4th. Prosperity to the Worshipful Company of Girdlers.

" 5th. The Master and Wardens drink of a Loving Cup to you, gentlemen. Strangers, you are all heartily welcome."

This old custom of drinking from the loving cup is still honoured at Girdlers' Hall, and the cup circulates round all the tables, the man who has just drunk standing up and guarding the back of the man drinking, and so carrying out the old idea of protecting the latter from being stabbed, which old custom is said by some to be carried out in commemoration of the murder of the Saxon Prince, Edward the Martyr, in A.D. 979, related by William of Malmesbury, who states that the prince being thirsty in the course of his hunting, came to Corfe Castle in Dorsetshire, the residence of his stepmother, Elfrida, and called for something to drink, and whilst in the act of drinking out of the cup was stabbed in the back by her order, and died from the wound, but whether the custom is really derived as far back as that it is impossible to say, but at some of the old City Companies to this day the dagger is still handed round with the loving cup.

Curiously enough there is no mention of the toast of the ladies being honoured, although it could hardly have been omitted.

The Court seem to have been very conservative over the bill of fare, although occasionally sweeping changes were introduced. Thus, in 1720, there is a Court order to the effect, " That the same dinner be provided as last year on election day, excepting only that English Hams be provided instead of Oysters and sausages." This minute may have had something to do with the tradition that the Company is addicted to saddles of pork, and regards that dish with something akin to the same affection as Charles Lamb did sucking pig. Certainly the tradition is widely credited, and to this day the joint is always provided at the Livery dinner if in season.

The Company in those days dined off pewter, like the rest of the world, and they seem to have had a goodly store of this, and there are constant references in the old cash books to the purchase and sale of this metal :

" 1654. To Mr. Jackson, Pewterer, for 244 pounds weight of Pewter, 94 pounds, whereof was abated for old pewter exchanged at 2*d.* a pound, and

150 pounds at 13½*d.*, which together amounts to £9 04*s.* 05*d.*" [1]

"For carrying of the said Pewter by severall burdens from and to the Hall, 01*s.* 03*d.*"

The arrangement of the flowers differed also somewhat from our present method, each man being provided with a nosegay, and the bill for six dozen of these came to 3*s.* There was also a payment for rushes, with which the floor was strewed preparatory to every feast, the item reading, "for two flaskets of strawings 3/6."

The Cook was a very important personage in those days, and kept a sharp lookout on his office, and in 1626 one of the stewards having ventured to employ a Mr. Ellis to dress two of the quarterly feasts, the Company's cook, Mr. Thomas Smith, "procured Mr. Ellis to be fined twenty shillings or thereabouts at Cookes Hall." This exasperated the Court when they heard it, and "It was ordered that the said Thomas Smith shall pay all such fine and charges as shall be imposed upon the said Mr. Ellis for the dressing of the said dinners, or otherwise he shall no longer remain Cook to this Company." In 1661 the Cook was censured by the Court on account of several complaints made against him by the old Stewards, and also of some unhandsome and disrespectful

---

[1] This takes a little working out, but the audit committee of that day was equal to it.

words spoken by him relating to some of the Assistants.

In addition to his pay, the Cook was allowed a perquisite of 5s. at each election dinner for aprons.

Smoking was introduced early in Girdlers' Hall, the first time the entry appearing being when Charles II made his state progress through the City in 1660, and the bill for two pounds of tobacco amounted to 5s., with another item of 4s. 6d. for burning three gross of pipes. After this date it appears pretty regularly. Subsequently, however, smoking was not permitted, but has been revived again in recent years, and is now allowed to be indulged in after the loyal toasts have been honoured, but not in the ancient form of clay pipes and churchwardens. The old time Girdlers were a convivial set of men, and nothing shows this more clearly than a study of the former Renter Wardens' accounts, a few extracts from which are here given as samples of what occurs nearly every year :

" To paid for two bucks given to ye Stewards for the amendment of the Election Dinner, £14 0s. 0d."

The following two items, curiously enough, come next to each other year after year. Could they have been the foundation of Mr. Punch's joke ?

"Paid for beer and ale at the Audit Day, 14/6.

"Paid for mops and brooms the same day, 1/6."

Another old custom now vanished for many years is shown by the following:

"Paid for fower bottles of Hypocras carried home to the newe Master and Wardens wives, 12/."

This was continued long after the Fire of London, only the beverage was changed from hypocras to sack.

One more item and we can drop the drink question:

"Payd for sugar and nutmegs for Grate Cupps, 9/10."

The dessert question is constantly referred to in the minute books, this being revived and abolished according to the fluctuations of the finances of the Company. In 1697 mention is first made of oranges and lemons, for which the Company paid 7s. 6d. Curiously enough, they seem to have had a great liking for "Carrawayes," which they constantly bought at the rate of 2s. 4d. for two pounds; and sugar-loaf is an item that appears regularly at a cost of 1s., whilst a pound of fine sugar is entered at 8d. Lunching off geese seems to have been a favorite pastime, and in 1698 three could be had for 9s. 6d. Another luxury highly esteemed was radishes, for which the cash book has several entries.

Sometimes the Company came in for an un-expected dinner, or at least "a dryncking," owing to the death of one of the members who was buried from the Hall, which was such a common event that most of the Companies kept a state pall, with the arms of the mystery worked on in a very resplendent manner. There are several entries of this custom in the Girdlers' books, and those who attended the funeral afterwards came back to the Hall to pass the rest of the day in feasting or "a dryncking" (recreation was the word euphemistically used), for which the dead man had thoughtfully provided the money. A good example is that of William Ettes, who by his will, dated 1550, left "to the Wardens and Fellowship of Gyrdelers of the City of London twenty shillings for a recreation among such as should attend his exequies in their liveries," but very often money was left for a regular feast, such as Christopher Parris in 1633, who left a dinner for the whole Company, but at length these funeral recreations were abolished, as they became somewhat of a scandal, owing to the behaviour of some of those who attended, and in 1694 the Court made an order that in future the Hall should not be let out for any burial under a penalty of £5.

During the time of the Plague the dinners were very much cut down, and for several years the Company were obliged to refrain from dining at all. Thus in 1625 a letter was read from the Lord Mayor to the Master and Wardens, " whereby he entreated them in respect of God's heavy visitation of the plague, they should forbear all manner of feasting or revelling, or making of public dinners at their Common Hall or elsewhere during the time of the visitation, and that they would be pleased in respect of the money thereby spared out of their pity and charity to send forth into the Chamber of London their large and liberal contributions to be expended in the relief of such poor people who are afflicted and not able to help themselves."

On consideration of this letter it was resolved that in respect of the great danger of infection they might incur by having public meetings or searches, it was thought meet there should be no quarterly dinner at Michaelmas and Bartholomew's day for the Livery or Yeomanry, or any searches made unless it please the Lord to cease his heavy visitation before that time.

Five years later the Lord Mayor sent another precept to the same effect, but the Court was not so disposed then " to forbear all manner of revelling," and the following rather involved order was made, that no dinner take place on election day, but that they hoped that the Lord Mayor would stay his hand and allow them to meet for the purpose of electing the several officers as usual, but at the same time provision be made for a small dinner or banquet for those who attended on that day. Yet again another precept was received from the Lord Mayor urging them to be moderate, and so matters continued. However, in 1666, it was ordered "that as no Feast had been held for the Livery on the preceding Lord Mair's Day in consequence of the sad contagion, the same having been postponed, the stewards were ordered to procure two bucks for the dinner on August 16th." This, as it happened, was the last dinner held in the old hall, or in fact anywhere for some years, as "the dreadfull and dismall fire" occurring next month it was ordered that no dinner be held for five years, and the money saved to help to rebuild the Hall.

The great day at Girdlers' Hall has ever been and still is election day, when the Company assemble for the purpose of choosing the Master, Wardens, and officials. This is usually on or about St. Lawrence's day, early in August. The whole of the Court and Livery being assembled, and the election being carried out in accordance with the ancient formalities, the Company then march in a body to church (St. Lawrence, Jewry), there to hear a sermon, for which a special fee of 3s. 5d. per annum was left by a pious benefactor many centuries ago. This is one of the oldest and most picturesque of the ceremonies, and formerly was carried out with great pomp, the Company with the Master and Wardens at the head marching in a body in their gowns, the parson marching with them, and the church and Company's officials attending with their maces and staves. In addition to this they were accompanied by a band of musicians, and in certain periods of our history with candles or lights, and thus resplendent marched through the streets singing a processional hymn, but although a little of this survives to the present day, the musicians and the candles and the hymn have all long ago vanished, and the ceremony is cut down to ideas more in consonance with the spirit of these modern times. During the time of the service the "music had dined with the servants," in accordance with an order of the Court (one can imagine them rushing back to the Hall from the church door in a very different fashion from which they had left it a few minutes before, those carrying the heavy instruments making desperate efforts to keep up with their fellows). At the close of the service the Company marched back to the Hall to dine. The Master and Wardens were crowned after dinner. This crowning is still carried out with a certain amount of ceremony, which has been somewhat revived of late years. A procession is formed with the Beadle carrying his mace and robed leading the music (usually trumpeters from the Grenadier Guards); then the Porter with the crowns on a cushion, followed by the Clerk, and behind him the Butler with the loving cup. This procession marches up the centre of the Hall to the Master, and the Clerk thereupon places the crown on his head, calling his name, and crowning him Master of the Girdlers' Company for the year ensuing. The Butler then hands him the loving cup, with which he pledges the Company. The same ceremony is then gone through with the Wardens, and the procession returns the way it came.

It is not known how many hundreds of years this ceremony has been carried out, but Mr. St. John Hope on examining the crowns gave it as his opinion that they are sixteenth-century workmanship, so that it looks as though the custom dated back as far as the incorporation charter of the Company, and although no specific mention of it is made in any of the minute books, still there is in one of the Company's old cash books, dated 1550, a note as to one of these crowns, so that they were evidently in use at that date. The crowns in question are made of velvet and silk, and have the outside handsomely embroidered with gold wire, and the figure of St. Lawrence is also worked on them and many gridirons, and also the national emblems of the rose and the thistle. They were originally gold and blue, but the velvet has long since lost its colour and has gone quite brown, although the silk of the crown is still a bright yellow. This ceremony, or rather a re-hearsal of it, has been photographed lately by Sir Benjamin Stone, M.P., and added to his collection of photographs of English customs. In former times the Company ended up election day by a grand ball, and musicians were provided "for the ladies' accommodation to dance." The ball was opened at six o'clock (after the Hall had been cleared of the election dinner débris), and by an order of the Court no one was admitted thereto until that hour.

We read a good deal in old books of the some-what free and easy manners and behaviour of our ancestors on festive occasions like this, and they are reported to have done many things, and to have shown their gaiety sometimes in a manner which would cause grave offence in these days, but I do not think that this charge could be justly laid to the Girdlers, as the Court evidently took a lot of trouble over this ball and the behaviour of those who attended, and some such order as the following is pretty frequent in the minute books : " It is the intent and desire of the Court that the elegance and order of the entertainment may as near as possible" resemble that of the preceding year, and it is fair to assume from this that the conduct and behaviour of the ancient Girdlers, their wives and daughters, and the guests who accompanied them on these occasions were both decorous and seemly, and anything like the manners of the Knights of the Bath, who, on one occasion when they visited the City, carried themselves insolently, "but specially in putting citizens wives to the squeak,"[1] would probably not have been tolerated for an instant at Girdlers' Hall. So particular were the Court to do the thing handsomely that in 1744 they resolved that, "the Company being unable to support the usual grandeur and dignity of the election day, do abolish the ball." They, however, underrated the power of the sex, and at the next Court the order was rescinded, and "it was resolved that there be a ball in the evening as usual, with a suitable band of music and proper entertainment for the ladies." This is the only example I have found in the minute books where the order of one Court has been reversed by an order of the next, and in fact it is very seldom indeed that an order of Court is reversed after it has once passed. The ladies, however, went one better than this, as at the next Court but one an order was passed that at the next election dinner a ball take place after dinner as usual, but in 1760 the Court determined to hold all future meetings at a tavern instead of at the Hall, and thus abolished the ball and the presence of the ladies, and the former at any rate has never been revived. Another favourite form of recreation at

[1] London and the Kingdom, Sharpe.

Girdlers' Hall was the indulgence in suppers, but in 1633 a precept was received from the Lord Mayor "prohibiting the making of suppers at the Common Hall by those who call themselves countrymen," "it being a great consumption of victuals, and consequently affecting the poor of the Cittie," and it was ordered that in the future no such meetings be allowed.

Lord Mayor's day was another great day with the Company, who met very early in the morning on this occasion, and having all breakfasted together at the Hall, were accustomed to attend on the Lord Mayor in their barge, unless the state of their finances did not permit it, and there are many old precepts from Lord Mayors entered in the minute book as to this, enjoining the Company to attend. One in particular, dated 1650, orders that a barge should be prepared, with the banner of the arms of the Commonwealth in the place of those of the late King, whereupon the Court ordered a barge to be prepared to hold forty persons, and the account runs as follows :

	£	s.	d.
Hire of Barge	4	5	0
To the Trumpeters . . .	1	10	0
To the Drums and Fifes . . .	0	6	0
Yellow and Watchett ribbons for the Watermen, Drums, and Fifes .	1	4	0
	7	5	0

Times, however, soon changed, and a few years after, namely in 1662, a precept received from the Lord Mayor was read "Injoining thereby for a preparation for the King and Queen, and other great personages, passage from Hampton Court to Whitehall, with their Barge, Streamers, and other ornaments, for so great a solemnity." Whereupon it was ordered that care be taken that a good barge be provided for the Livery for that day, and that Mr. Body, who formerly served this Company for many years, do give notice to the Master and Wardens of what he has provided, and receive their approbation thereof from the Master and Wardens, and that this be forthwith done, that the Company may be in readiness against the day, whensoever it may be appointed.

This attending on the Lord Mayor on his day of election was a duty always religiously observed by the Company, but in 1738, on the receipt of the usual precept, the Court considered the foregoing matter, and laid a remonstrance with humble submission before the Lord Mayor and Court of Aldermen, stating that whilst the Company was sensible of the honour and respect due to the Lord Mayor, and are greatly desirous of contributing all in their power to support the dignity of the high office as far as is consistent with the welfare and honour of this ancient Company, but they are suffering from debt and not able to defray the expense of such attendance, their estates are small, and some charged with, and some wholly applied to charitable uses (which the Company religiously observe), their almshouses are so out of repair as to require rebuilding. The Stewards fine too heavy for some of their members, so that it has been reduced, and the Company are doing all in their power to reduce their expenses and improve their condition. The Company hope soon to be able to support the expense of such attendance, when they assure the Lord Mayor and Court of Aldermen that they will readily, cheerfully, and constantly perform the said honour.

The only result of this petition was that the Master was summoned before the Lord Mayor, who seems to have rated the Company soundly, and insisted absolutely that the Master, Wardens, Court, and Livery should attend, and when the day drew near, a summons was delivered from the Lord Mayor and Court of Aldermen requiring the Company to attend in a proper manner the public procession, and they had to do so.

Royal progresses have always been honoured by the Company with their " best formalities," and those members who did not actually wait in person or ride in the procession attended at the stands erected in Cheapside. All the Companies erected their stands at their own fixed spot, the place assigned to the Girdlers being at the corner of

Gutter Lane, and they were erected and pulled down as required, the Company usually entering into a contract with a carpenter for the erection of "a fashionable and substantial stand" at a cost of 40s. Here the Company attended "with all their formalities," with their trophies carried by the Whifflers, who were decked out with yellow and watchet ribbons for the occasion, and sometimes they regaled themselves with music, as on the day of the entry of George I into London, when the price of the stand was agreed at £6, "the music if good to be £4."

The attendances of the Guilds on these royal progresses goes very far back, and it will be remembered how in the reign of Edward IV the Company attended on the entry of the Queen to her coronation.

In 1654 the cash book shows, "To Piggott, carpenter, for work done by him in setting up and lengthening the rayles, and making of seats for the Livery, when his Highness the Lord Protector came through the Cittie."

A long account appears in the minute books of the state observed by the Company on the occasion of Charles II's entry into the City, when it was ordered that "the stands be in readiness against His Majesty's riding through this his Cittie of London, and for the attendance of fourteen persons of this Company to attend on horseback at His

Majesty's entrance into this his Cittie, apparelled in velvet or plush, with their chains of gold, and all things answerable thereunto, and that Mr. Chambers, the present Master, Mr. Warden Taylor, and Mr. Warden Rush, with eleven others, whose names are given, should be the persons to attend, according to the precept, and that everyone of them should have a footman to attend on them apparelled in watchett cloth trimmed with yellow ribbands, with new hatts, new stockings, and new shoes, to be provided at the Companies charge, and Mr. Warden Taylor and Mr. Warden Rush were desired to take care for providing the said cloth, ribbands, and other necessaries," and it was also agreed that "a new Banner of His Majesty's Arms, and another of the Cittie, should be provided against the day of His Majesty's said entrance, and Richard Lynton (the porter), was appointed to carry the Banner of the Company's Arms before the said Gentlemen, to be arrayed in the same manner as the footmen, and it was also thought meete that six young men of the Company should attend on the rest of the Livery, that should be at the Company's standings the next day."

John Evelyn in his diary mentions the grand state observed by the City Companies on this occasion :

"May 29th. This day his Majestie Charles II came to London, after a sad and long exile, and calamitous suffering both of the King and Church, being 17 yeares. This was also his birthday, and with a triumph of above 20,000 horse and foote brandishing their swords and shouting with inexpressible joy; the wayes strew'd with flowers, the bells ringing, the streets hung with tapistry, fountains running with wine, the Mayor, Aldermen, and all the Companies in their liveries, chaines of gold and banners, Lords and Nobles clad in cloth of silver, gold, and velvet, the windowes and balconies well set with ladies, trumpets, music, and myriads of people flocking even so far as from Rochester, so as they were seven houres in passing the Citty, even from 2 in the afternoone till 9 at night. I stood in the Strand and beheld it, and blessed God, and all this was don without one drop of bloud shed, and by that very army which rebelled against him; but it was the Lord's doing, for such a Restauration was never mentioned in any history, antient or modern, since the returne of the Jews from the Babylonick captivity, nor so joyfull a day and so bright ever seene in the Nation, this hapning when to expect or effect it was past all human policy."

Like the rest of the world the Company nearly did for themselves altogether on this occasion, as, in addition to the expenditure in all this arraying in velvet or plush apparel, they had to pay the sum of £42, their share of the credit for £3,000 voted by the City for defraying the charge of His Majesty's entertainment at Guildhall, and the Company were so hard put to it for money that the Master had to come to the rescue, and very generously lent them £200.

The banners mentioned are still preserved in the Company's old oak chest, but they are absolutely in rags and beyond repair, and crumble up in the hand when touched.

A very few years afterwards, namely in 1665, the Company again appeared in "all their formalities," the occasion being when "the Russia Ambassador" was received, when they deputed certain of their number to join with the other Companies in riding out against him ("to ride out against" was the phrase always used), whilst the rest of the Company betook themselves to their stands.

There have been many similar occasions in which the Company appeared in all their formalities, but the last time they took part in any royal procession was when they were represented in the procession on the occasion of the public entry into the City of Her Royal Highness the Princess Alexandra of Denmark, the affianced bride of His Royal Highness the Prince of Wales, on the 7th March, 1863.

In the midst of the lighter side of their lives, the Company did not forget the religious, and there was an old custom, now quite died out, for the whole of the Court and Livery to attend at St. Paul's Church four times a year, and there listen to a sermon, and the item appears regularly in the cash book:

" For a forme for the Maister and Wardens and Livery to sit on at Pawles on 18th September to hear the sermon being a feast day and for the almsman there, 6/-."

This custom, however, began to die out and cease when the art itself decayed, so that the only service attended by the Company now in its official capacity is the service they attend once a year on election day at their mother church, St. Lawrence, Jewry, and which custom, as has been shown before, has probably been in vogue and goes back as far as the beginning of the Company itself.

After reading the above chapter it will be seen that the old time Girdler's life was much more centred in his guild than is possible under present conditions, and that he practically passed the whole of his life within a few hundred yards of the Hall, beginning with his being bound apprentice, and possibly ending up by his being buried from there; and it will further be observed that formerly there were many more occasions on which the Company met together for the purposes of either work or pleasure, so that it is no great matter for surprise that the tie between the various members of the body was so strong, and that many old customs and ideas crept in and flourished from one decade to another which were faithfully handed down by each successive generation of Girdlers, and although of necessity the greater part of these old customs have died out with the decay of the art and the change in the manners of the age, yet we still retain, and jealously cling to the few that have survived the general wreck, and perhaps one of the greatest pleasures in belonging to these old City guilds is the participating in the ancient customs and ideas which serve in some manner to bring back to our minds the days when the Company carried out its original functions in respect to its trade, and was a sort of little republic in itself, and which customs, going back as they do to the time " when the memory of man runneth not to the contrary," have now acquired a prescriptive sanction, so that the Company are right in not allowing them lightly to drop, even if their original significance has somewhat died out and is no longer of vital importance.

CAP. VII

FINANCIAL

That which her slender waist confined
Shall now my joyful temples bind.
It was my heaven's extremest sphere,
The pale which held that lovely dear.
My joy, my grief, my hope, my love,
Did all within this circle move.
A narrow compass! and yet there
Dwelt all that's good and all that's fair.
Give me but what that ribbon bound,
Take all the rest the sun goes round.
            " *On a Girdle,*" *Edmund Waller,* 1605-1687.

IN considering the financial side to the history of the Girdlers' Company, we shall find that, like many of the other Guilds, there have been times when the Company has had to struggle hard to live and to pay its way, and this not so much from any extravagance or want of forethought on the part of the Company itself, as from the rapacity and greed of others, for it must be borne in mind that a large portion of the world looks upon a City Company as an institution to which they can

176

fairly appeal for funds and aid for nearly every conceivable cause, and no matter for what reason money is wanted, the City Company, like Mr. W. S. Gilbert's bottle, is considered "fair game."[1]

It will be remembered that the very first knowledge we have of the Company is a record of how they were forced to undergo the penalty of a fine of twenty-five marks at the hands of King Henry II for carrying on their business without a licence, which it is submitted they were perfectly justified in doing, and, as we shall see later on, this is only one of many instances in which the Company were forced to pay money to the higher authorities on some pretext or other.

It is impossible to say at this distance of time what the financial situation of the Company was in its earlier stages of existence, and even if we knew their income it would hardly be a fair criterion of the position, as there were so many ways formerly, especially in feudal times, of taxing people without exacting money, namely, through the medium of services, by which means a good deal could be got out of a man without any money actually passing; thus in 1314, when Edward II was defending the town of Berwick-on-Tweed, he wrote to the City of London for assistance, and in response the City sent 120 arbalasters to assist the king, and the guilds were called upon to assist

[1] "A Bottle I think fair Game."—*Bab Ballads.*

in providing these, and one of these men at least was provided and equipped by the Company, as his name is given as " Nicholas Horn, Zeynturer."

Another favourite method of exacting money from people was by means of what was called " Benevolences," a practice instituted by Edward IV, and followed by many of our later kings and queens, especially Queen Elizabeth, who was very partial to this form of raising money. This was a system of obtaining money compulsorily whilst pretending it was given by the donor of his own free will and initiative, and was applied not only to private people, but also others, such as the City Guilds, and it is recorded how, in 1355, John de Cauntebrigg, Chamberlain, has received from divers mysteries for an offering to present to the Lord the King of England, towards carrying on the French wars, from the Zonars, £6 13s. 4d. Historians differ so much as to the value of money in those times, that it is difficult to say what that would now represent, but taking it at twenty times the present value, which I think is a fair estimate, this would amount to £133 6s. 8d. A very common way of exacting services from the Companies was by making them carry out repairs to the City walls, and also to attend to the needs of the river, as in 1422, Parliament having enacted that all the weirs or rydells in the Thames between Staines, Gravesend, and Queenborough should be destroyed, the Mayor and Common Council ordained that two men from each of the twenty-six crafts should go out with the Mayor for this business. With the Brewers were joined six other crafts, viz., the Girdlers, Fletchers, Salters, Barbers, Dyers, and Tallow Chandlers, who were all to go in one barge. The Fletchers excusing themselves as being too busy on account of preparing "artillery" for the king, who was then in France, were permitted to find substitutes and make payment.

In addition to taxes and fines imposed by order of the King and Parliament, and which fall more under the head of public or natural taxes, notice must also be taken of sums paid in connection with the City itself, such as to the Guildhall, and which are more in the nature of local taxes, and one of the earliest of these I have been able to find occurs during the mayoralty of Sir John Shaa in 1501 in connection with the building of the kitchen of the Guildhall, to which the various Fellowships of their own agreement subscribed according to their means, and "the Gyrdlers amount was £iij vjˢ viijd," and since then, with the exception of the interval caused by the Fire, the annual dinner of the Lord Mayor and Sheriffs has been held at the Guildhall.

The providing of coal and corn was another

duty imposed upon the City Companies, and can best be understood from the following extract from Northwick's " History of London ":

" For a constant supply of sea-coal for the use of the poor in times of scarcity, and to defeat the combinations of coal dealers, the several City Companies undermentioned were ordered to purchase and lay up yearly between Lady Day and Michaelmas the following quantities of coal, which in dear times were to be vended in such manner and at such price as the Lord Mayor and Court of Aldermen should by written precept direct, so that the coals should not be sold at a loss:

The Mercers, 488 chaldrons
The Girdlers, 105   ,,
The Glaziers,   6   ,,

These show the largest and smallest quantities laid up in 1665."

The corn duty started earlier, and in the following manner. In 1545 a great quantity of foreign wheat was sent over to England, and the Companies were called upon to assist in purchasing it. " The Common Council agreed that my lorde mayor should immediately call the Wardens of all the substancyall Companies before him and move theym for the lone of some money to pay for the wheate that has now come from beyonde the sea The Companies obeyed and next day paid the quotas they were rated at. The Gyrdelers xx£."

The Lord Mayor and Aldermen were also ordered to arrange terms "with sad honeste and discrete persons for the lyke provision to be made in other places of the realme."

This corn was kept at the Bridge House, where there were granaries, mills, and ovens, and the Company's books have many entries in connection with this, from which it appears that the Company's rateable proportion on a requisition of 10,000 quarters to be provided by the City Companies, was 140 quarters well conditioned. Subsequently the Company, like many of the other guilds, built its own granary at the Bridge House, and regular items appear in the cash book year after year in connection with this.

"To John Wildynge, Beadle, for charges disbursed by him in turning and screening the Companies Corne in their Granary in the Bridge House from 1st day of July to last day of December, £5 03s. 07d."

This went on for over 100 years, but in 1688, when a precept was received ordering the Company to send in their usual quantity of corn into the granary, the Company were in such financial straits that the Court "empowered and requested the Master and Wardens to appear before the Lord Mayor and represent the utter inability of the Company in the present position of their funds to contribute," and I do not find that the Girdlers ever did contribute anything to the corn duty after this date.

Bill of adventure was another form of inducing the Companies to part with their money, and the Girdlers adventured on several undertakings, all of which are faithfully set out in the cash book in what was called " the grand accompt."

" Item two Bills of adventure under the Seale of the Virginia Company for so much adventured by this Company towards the plantation there, £50.

" Item divers acquittances from the Chamberlain and his clerks for the receipt of the sum of 570 paid at severall times by this Company for and towards the plantation in Ireland by force of severall acts of Comon Councill and precepts from the Lord Mayor, £570."

These bills of adventure were a favourite method adopted to induce the various Companies to subscribe to certain undertakings of a more or less public character, of which the Virginia Company may be taken as a very fair example, this being a company started to colonize Virginia, named after Queen Elizabeth, in whose reign it was discovered, and which got so badly in need of assistance that in 1608 a Lord Mayor's precept was issued to the Companies and was sent round with a letter from the Council of Virginia. Herbert, in his history of the twelve great Companies, gives an account of this, and states " that people were induced to emigrate there, and to entice them were promised meat, drink, and clothing, with a house and garden for the maintenance of a family, and a portion of land likewise for them and their posterity of 100 acres each." Very much on the same sort of principle as is applied in Canada at the present time, and just as in Canada the emigrants often find the need of wives to keep their houses in order, so the same need was found in Virginia, and many young women were later on sent out, and also numerous children, so that the colony in time prospered, and it was towards this object that the Girdlers adventured £50.

The plantation of Ireland however, was far and away the most important undertaking adventured upon by this Company, although it must be confessed that here again the money was wrung from them rather than given willingly; the idea was first submitted to the Livery Companies in 1609, and they were told that by assisting in the plantation they would not only be doing a work acceptable unto God, but one which would be at once honourable and profitable unto themselves, and the King offered to the City of London the City of Derry with adjacent territory and certain advantageous rights as to customs and admiralty jurisdiction, as an inducement to them to subscribe. A precept was issued to certain of the more important Guilds, and ultimately this Company paid

as much as £570 16s., and were grouped with the
Skinners, the Stationers, and the Whitebakers,
and a share of the plantation was allotted to them
out of the particular estates conveyed by deed
dated 5th June, 1663, by the Irish Society to the
Skinners' Company, and called after them the Pellipar estates. The first instalment of this money
was spent on fortifying Derry with walls and gates,
so that subsequent moneys had to be raised for
the plantation of the estate itself, and the Company paid their share of this also, and the Company have retained their share, which is com-
puted at $\frac{137}{1200}$, or received its equivalent value
down to the present time, so that in respect to
this they were more fortunate than was the case
over the Virginia adventure. As may be readily
supposed the troublous times of King Charles and
his struggle with the Parliamentary forces was
one of the most difficult times for the Company,
so far as its financial history goes, and no matter
which side for the moment had the ascendency,
the City Companies had to pay the piper, and
were called upon to find the money on some excuse or other. The demands began in 1628, when
a precept was received from the Lord Mayor
setting out the terms of the "royal contract," in
which the City covenanted to advance King
Charles £120,000 in two instalments of £60,000,
and calling upon the Company to pay £600, their

share according to their ancient proportion of corn, and after debate it was ordered that the money should be borrowed under the seal of the Company at £7%, and also the Company's plate should be handed over as security. Shortly afterwards a further demand of £200 was made, and the Court, bearing in mind the fate of imprisonment inflicted on the Wardens of certain of the other Companies who refused to pay, again borrowed the money and met the demand. In 1634, when King Charles raised the demand for ship money in the City, the Company paid the amount assessed on them without demur, although the City did its best to escape the payment, and in the compromise made with the King in 1638 on the forfeiture of the Irish estates for alleged breaches of the Charter, another £200 was paid after several meetings, although on the first demand from the Lord Mayor the Court refused to pay on the ground that the proportion asked of the Company was in excess of their proper rate.

The Company had now pretty well come to the end of its tether, and when, in 1642, both houses of Parliament applied to the City Companies for a loan of £100,000 towards "the relief and preservation of the kingdom of Ireland," and "the speedy supply of the great and urgent necessities of this kingdom," the Company had no money to pay. The usual precept was received from the

Lord Mayor, and the Company was asked to contribute £1,000, their ancient proportion according
to their rating for the corn tax, and they were
promised interest on their money at the rate of
£8% per annum, and after considerable debate the
Court ordered that the sum of £1,000 should be
advanced, and as the Company had no money
towards the amount, it was resolved to raise the
whole amongst the several members of the Livery,
and such others as the Master and Wardens
should suggest as willing to advance the same on
loan, and the amount was ultimately raised by the
members of the Court themselves in sums varying
from £10 to £100.

Unfortunately for the Company this was by no
means the end of their financial troubles, as next
year a letter was read from the Lord Mayor
" whereby it was intimated that his Lordship, with
the Aldermen and Common Council then assembled, being sensible of the great and imminent
danger of the Cittie by the near approach of the
King's forces, and of the great and pressing
necessity for money at present for the safety and
defence thereof," had resolved to call upon the
Livery Companies for the sum of £50,000, and
the letter further went on to impress the Company
with the urgency of the matter, and ended up by
asking for £700, the Company's ancient proportion according to the corn tax, to be paid to the

treasurer at Guildhall within a few days. This demand came on top of another made a short time before for money to be spent on the City walls and defences, which the Company had managed to satisfy with the help of members of the Court. This being taken into consideration it was ordered that £500, according to the Company's ancient proportion, should be raised and lent, and to meet this it was ordered that such plate as belonged to the Company remaining unsold should be sold, and should there still remain a deficiency, the amount to be borrowed on the Common Seal of the Company. Accordingly the plate was sold, and the surplus, after paying off what it had been formerly mortgaged for, amounted to £150, and this and no more was paid into the Guildhall, as the Court were unable to raise any more money on their Common Seal. This was naturally not accepted in discharge by the Guildhall authorities, and a general meeting of the Company was called, whereat there appeared not more than ten of the Livery, nor about as many of the Yeomanry. Whereupon the Wardens, accompanied by two members of the Court, went round to the houses and shops of the absentees and compelled them to attend, and when the whole Company was assembled, the Master stated "That the Master and Wardens were, on Thursday last, warned before the Lord Mayor and Court of Aldermen, to bring in the remainder of the £700 (which is £550 to make up the Company's proportion towards the £50,000 to be lent by Act of Common Council upon the Citties seal in bonds) to-morrow morning, or to return the answer of this Company, together with a list of the names of the Master, Wardens, Assistants, and Livery of this Company."

Now this meeting was to consider of the business, and to know what answer the Master and Wardens shall return, and to this end they had warned all the Livery. For in all probability, if the Company return the names without the money, the Court of Aldermen will rate everyone to pay his rate. The above was taken into serious consideration, whether the Company should rate themselves or the Court of Aldermen, or what course should be taken. Whereupon, after a full and serious debate and due consideration, it was ordered that the names of the Master, Wardens, and Livery shall be presented together with this answer:

This Company have paid all other subsidies, weekly payments, and assessments required.

They have lent £1,000 towards Ireland and the affairs of this kingdom.

They have lent all their arms to the state.

They have sold their plate, and carried £150 into Guildhall towards their proportion of the

£50,000, which was all their plate would yield above what it was formerly mortgaged for.

They had endeavoured to take up money upon their Common Seal, and cannot have more, for that their lands are tyed for charitable purposes. Besides which they are indebted about £2,000, and have not money to repair their Common Hall, being very ruinous, nor to defray the ordinary necessary charges of the Company.

The return of this answer, with the names, must have had the effect of causing the Common Council to rate the members of the Company individually, as nothing more appears about it in the minute books, so that the Company escaped sequestration for this time. However the respite was not for long, as, in addition to all these payments, the Company was rated with a weekly payment of £8 for the Parliamentary army, and the Company now being without any money, and unable to borrow, began to fall behind with their payments, and eventually got as much as nineteen months into arrear; but when the rate had been twelve months unpaid, the Court had petitioned, and got the assessment reduced to £7 10s. a week, and the Company, by various means, including when the rate was first made, the sale of some plate, had managed to pay this demand. The plate, however, with these many demands on it, could not last for ever, and the collector from

Bassishaw began to call more and more frequently to demand payment. It was impossible to pay without money, however, and the members of the Court had helped the Company so frequently on former emergencies out of their own moneys that they were unable to come forward with any more, and their own taxes at that time must have been very heavy, so that on the 6th December, 1648, a warrant was read to the Court from the Committee for the advance of the army requiring the Company to pay their arrears forthwith, amounting to £96 in all, and requiring the amount to be paid on the Wednesday following, otherwise the Company would be returned to the Committee for sequestration.

The Court resolved that they should, in pursuance of their faithful respect to the public, pay to the collector the sum of £9 9s. 11d., which was according to the greatest valuation that could be made of the Hall after the rate of £40 per annum. This amount was accordingly paid, and next month a warrant was read from Thomas Martin requiring the Master and Wardens to attend the Committee of Sequestration at Camden House, Maiden Lane, to pay all assessments, otherwise to be sequestrated according to ordinance of Parliament. The Master and Wardens accordingly attended, and though they begged for a respite, the Company was sequestrated, and their revenues were collected by the Parliamentary Committee.

Once more the Court fell into serious debate, and although several members, as usual, patriotically came forward, they could not raise sufficient money, and ultimately the old device of summoning yeomen to take up their livery had to be resorted to, and over thirty were summoned and paid the fine, and after about two years, by this means, and by the help of members of the Court, the arrears of taxes were paid off, and the Company was rescued from the clutches of the Committee.

There have been several other occasions on which the Company has been called upon to pay large sums of money, only one more of which I propose to mention, and that was in the year 1666, when the City made an offer of a ship to the King called " The Loyal London," and a precept was issued by the Lord Mayor to the Livery Companies to " excite and persuade " their members to subscribe to the undertaking. The amount asked for from this Company was £140, and was with the greatest difficulty subscribed, and the members of the Court again had to come to the assistance of the Company. Pepys has a good deal to say about this ship in his Diary, and it will be remembered that when her guns were tried at first they all burst.

The above extracts show pretty forcibly what a

struggle the Company had at times to keep its head above water, and it is also abundantly clear that if the struggle was severe the patriotism of the Court was equal to the occasion. And there are two or three instances in the minute books besides the ones given above when the Court have come to the rescue of the Company on critical occasions like these, when they were temporarily pressed for money.

A study of the Company's old account books will, perhaps, give a clearer idea of the internal workings of the Company than even the old minute books. These old general accounts go back as far as the year 1654 (although one of the Charity account books is older by one hundred years), and were known as "The Grand Accompt," and in some years are most beautifully written and kept. They contain the whole of the Company's financial transactions set out year by year, it being one of the duties of the clerk to make out this account, for which he was paid the sum of £1 in addition to his salary. The first items set out are the Company's rents, which vary from about £2 10s. to £12 per annum. The Company do not seem to have been very hard landlords, as in the year in question (1654) the book opens with some of the rents three years in arrear. Then comes a list of the fines for the year, which differ considerably both in amount and origin, thus:

"Annie Phillips, widowe, the some of sixtie

pounds, thirteene shillings and fowerpence for a fine of a lease granted to her of ye messuage wherein she dwelleth in the parish of St. Olave in Southwarke for one and twenty yeares, at the yearly rent of £12."

The next item being:

" Thomas Smart, almsman, beinge so much imposed upon him by order of Court as a mulct, for that his wife did use raylinge and unseemely words and accons towards John Bradley and his wife and some others of the almspeople, contrary to the article of the orders made for regulatinge of the almsmen and their wives, .05 . 00."

After that follow the names of the Master, and Wardens and Livery of the said Company, and of the sums of money received of them in their several quarterages. This was 4s. each, and some of them paid quarterly. This list shows that the total of the Court and Livery was only forty-three that year.

After the Court and Livery come " The names of such persons as have bin heretofore chosen of the Livery and are now sett out from the rest by reason of their continuall absences and withdrawinge themselves into the Country from appearance or otherwise, and yet ought to pay quarteridge." These numbered sixteen, and last come " the Decaied Livery," fortunately only two, and the Company bestowed on these sevenpence a week a-piece.

After this follow " The names of the Yeomanry or Freemen of the said Company, and the severall sums of money they paid for their quarteridge," and here it must be confessed there is an extra-ordinary laxity in collecting the money (or was it the impossibility of doing so?), as out of over 600 names only thirty-five had paid anything at all, and not one of these the full amount.

The next heading is "An account of ould debts and arrearages of quarteridge collected from some of the Livery and Yeomanry," and this varies from 3*d.* into pounds. " The Fynes received from various members because their apprentices were not enrolled according to an antient ordinance," amounted to nine at 10*s.* a-piece and one at 6*s.*

Fifty-five apprentices were bound that year for periods varying from seven to nine years, and each of them paid 2*s.* 6*d.*

Then the list of those who were made free during the year, and an account of their spoon money, which varied from " xs to nil", whilst others gave " 1 spoone."

There were altogether twenty-three made Free that year.

The disbursements of the Company are then set out, and some of them are rather interesting:

A charge of 2*s.* 6*d.* is allowed " to the Clerke for parchment to make two Livery Rolls and paper used on the audit day."

" Lewis Bromley, the Lord Mayor's Officer, for his fee this yeare 06 . 08."

And a like fee to Thomas Smith, Cooke.

On the other hand, the fee " for the yeare to the Parson of the Parish of St. Michaell Bassishaw" is only " 03 . 05," and his Clarke " 01 . 04."

But the scavenger of the said parish for his duties received " 05 . 04."

At the end of the reign of Queen Elizabeth the first poor law had been passed, and accordingly we find, " To the collectors for the poore of the said Parish for a yeare ended the 24th of June last past, £2 . 12 . 00."

Water rate is the next item and runs, " For the rente of the River water cominge into the Hall this yeare, £1 . 06 . 08." We do not know when this was first introduced into Girdlers' Hall, but it will be remembered that the project of the New River had been started in the reign of Queen Elizabeth, who had given the citizens of London authority to cut and bring to London a river from any part of Hertfordshire and Middlesex, which project was ultimately carried out by Maister Hugh Middleton, citizen and goldsmith, who united the two springs of Chadwell and Amwell and brought them to London, finally completing his labours, in spite of much opposition and derision, in 1613, so that the Girdlers had by this time probably had the advantage of this New River water for some years, and they have had it ever since.

A long list of pensions paid to "widdowes" and various "goodwives" follow, and then more taxes, being the amounts assessed on the Company's various properties for the army and navy tax, and they of course vary largely, according as the property was great or small, the amount levied on the Hall being £5 10s. There is then a further item in connection with the water rate, " To the collector of the Ward of Bassishaw for fower fifteenths assessed upon the Hall to bring the water to the conduits"; this was for bringing the water from the conduits into the Hall, but which conduits I am not quite certain, but it may have been the great conduit on the south side of Cheap. After that a long list of poor people who received benevolences at the rate of 2s. 6d. each is recorded, and then a fee of 2s. 6d. to "a soldier that served for the Company on the trayninge daye."

In those times it was customary for the Livery to dine with the Lord Mayor once a year, and the fees payable to his Sword-bearer, Butler, and Porters are regularly set out.

Mention has been made how a few years previously the Company had been sequestrated, and it appears that they had been rescued from this dilemma by the Mr. Taylor who had been both Clerk and afterwards Master, and an item of £20 appears for several years in repayment of money advanced by him on that occasion.

Shortly after appear a great number of items for the army tax, and then a curious item of "05.06 towards the charge of ye prosecucon of a divident of Plantation lande in Ireland, allotted to the Company by the Comme settinge at Grocers' Hall."

The next entry is domestic. " To Mr. Ferard Brasier, for exchange of a greate brasse Pann of the Companies, for the use of the Cooke the last yeare, the old one weyeinge $18\frac{1}{3}$ at 8, the new $22\frac{1}{2}$ at 18, 1.00.00."

	£	s.	d.
To the Armorer for cleaninge the Companies Arms this yeare .		06	08
Sume totall of the disbursements in ye yeare aforesaid . . .	387	0	$2\frac{1}{2}$
Sume totall of the Receipts in ye yeare aforesaid . . .	396	12	1
So there resteth due unto this Company	9	11	$10\frac{1}{2}$

"A list of Plate remayinge in the Treasury house of this Company" is shown on the next page, but it is very short, as all of the plate had been sold a few years previously, as mentioned above, and very little new had come in since then.

The Company's debts that year amounted to £433, so that it cannot be said their financial position was very sound.

It is recorded of a gentleman, one of Charles Dickens's creations, that he remarked " nothing's real except taxes, and they're very real indeed," and this is especially true when we come to go through the old account books of the Girdlers' Company and see what the Company paid for rates and taxes at different periods of their history, and, considering the smallness of their income, it must be confessed that at times the amounts were " very real indeed," and another point to be noted is the extraordinary obtuseness displayed by our former legislators in the imposing of their exactions. Everything that could conduce to health and sanitary convenience seems to have been the subject of taxation; thus at various times we find " the hearths," " the windows," and " the chimneys " all taxed, so that it is a wonder the race did not die out altogether from sheer suffocation in their endeavours to escape these various exactions.

The trophy tax was another item which hit the Company very heavily, and was introduced in the fourteenth year of Charles II, and the money collected went towards providing harness and the maintenance of the trained bands, and this was in addition to the money paid for the trained bands which had been instituted in Queen Elizabeth's time, and revived again some time about 1614, and in 1615 the Common Council ordered a fifteenth to be levied on the inhabitants of the City towards the

" defrayinge of all maner of charges to be disbursed in and about the trayninge and musteringe of men"; but now that the trained bands have died out, the tax is applied to the maintenance of the militia barracks in the City Road, where the City of London Regiment is stationed.

The expense of travelling is shown by the item of £9 3s. 2d., expended by the Clerk in 1660 in a journey to Rumney Marsh, to view the Company's land there, and colleƈt the rent.

A barrel of gunpowder about the same date cost £3 10s., and the Court cheerfully stowed six of these in the Company's store, laid under the Hall, and if they were there in 1666, they must have somewhat distraƈted the attention of those who were engaged in rescuing the Company's goods.

The Company also laid in pikes, muskets, swords, and hangers, at a cost of £9 16s.

There are many entries about this time of money paid to various members " on the sad occasion of their houses being inteƈted with the contagion, or to pay for the burial of those carried off by it."

If "blessings unnumbered follow in civilization's train," so also do a certain amount of evils, and one of the commonest is the pipes bursting, and among the entries for 1684 is a charge for 1s. 7d. for " the pipe being broke in the great frost";

thus we see that even this domestic calamity should be regarded in the nature of a time-honoured custom, and taken philosophically.

The state of the coinage in 1695 was evidently not all it should have been: "Payd for loss in putting off Guineas and clipt money received by the Company, £16." This is very heavy, but fortunately does not occur often, otherwise it would have been a very serious tax on the Company's income.

There are many curious items set out every year, such as small sums, "for the womens dyett at severall times for cleaning the Hall and Scouring the Company's Pewter," which varied each year between 6s. 6d. and 7s. 4d. Also "strong beere" and "small beere" was laid in for the workmen, and now and again an almsman got distracted, and was comforted with a pound; the soldiers, too, for powder and bullets received 6s. each, and even the smallest items are conscientiously set out, as they seem to have had no idea of petty cash, but enough has been given to show the general tenor and nature of these accounts.

The soldier who "served for the Company" evidently looked at life from a whimsical point of view, judging from the following in 1681:

"To so much payd for redemption of the Company's muskett pawned by Peter the soldier, 0.6.0."

The Company's clerk at the time of the Fire is thus picturesquely remembered after his death :

" To so much payd for Beere in Mr. Davis' lifetime, 03 . 04."

This was the Grand accompt, and it was signed regularly every year by about six or eight members of the Court, and once or twice we come across a member who was content with making his mark, and I cannot help thinking it shows rather a high sense of humour to ask a man to assist in auditing accounts who has not sufficient education to be able to set his signature at the end, and further, when we see the price of a bunch of radishes solemnly placed next to an item of several hundred pounds paid into the Chamber at the Guildhall, it is rather hard not to smile at such Arcadian simplicity, but perhaps we are not meant to take them too seriously, and it would I think, be better to regard them as accounts more strictly in a Pickwickian sense.

Before closing this chapter it may be as well to say a little about Royal Commissions, which the Company, like many others in the City of London, has had to submit to, and the earliest we know of was in the reign of Richard II, when all the Companies had to make a return of their lands, etc., but the first one mentioned in the minutes is in 1633, when the Court was informed that there was a quest of inquiry appointed for the viewing and search of the Bookes of the Companyes of the City of London, concerning sundry articles given them in charge; and it was thought fit, and ordered that the clerk should not show any of the Company's books to the said quest, and that when the said quest should come, he should acquaint the Master and Wardens, and state that in a short time they should have their answer, and that in the interim he cannot show anything, for that he hath taken an oath to the contrary.

The next Commission we have any knowledge of originated in 1833, when the clerk reported that he had received a communication from Sir Francis Palgrave, one of the Commissioners appointed to inquire as to the existing state of the several municipal corporations in England and Wales, and asking sixteen specific questions, and the clerk also reported that having obtained the Master's sanction to such a step, he did on the 17th of September attend Sir Francis Palgrave with papers and documents, furnishing the information required, when Sir Francis inspected the Charters of Charles I and James II, and further that Sir Francis also inspected the Charter of Queen Elizabeth, and retained it for the present, and at the same time handed to him a list of requisitions, and appointed 3rd October to attend him thereon. Whereupon the Court, taking the matter into consideration, resolved that the clerk be directed to comply with such requisitions, and to furnish the information the Commissioners required, and a Committee was also appointed to prepare the answers of the Company to the inquiries of the Royal Commission, who attended on the Commissioners, and delivered the replies after a letter had been sent to the Secretary, stating " That although the Court cannot but doubt the power of the Commissioners to call for such information, yet having nothing to conceal the Court are ready to direct the same to be furnished, provided the Commissioners will defray the expenses that must necessarily be incurred in preparing the information."

The next Commission, appointed in 1880, of which the late Earl of Derby was chairman, inquired into the inner life and the working of the various Companies to a far greater degree than the previous ones, and a study of the report issued at the end of the investigation will show how exhaustive and thorough the inquiry was, as the Committee's questions embraced every side of the Company's life from its foundation, and a very good idea of the financial position of the various Companies, with their ideals and ambitions, and the distribution of their funds and charities, the dates of their foundations and the connection with their various trades and crafts can be gathered by those who care to take the trouble to study the report of the Commissioners. This was the last general inquiry the Girdlers' Company have had to go through, and it has only to be added that they came through scathless, as they did through the previous ones.

CAP. VIII

THE HALL

Then God save the King! may we ever be staunch
To our worshipful Guild in its root and its branch,
And as we make merry and taste of the joys
Which the jolly old Girdlers have left for their boys,
May we never forget the Great Girdler above,
Who encircles the world with his Girdle of Love.

Friar John Lonarius.

"GIRDLERS HALL, a very handsome building with an open Court yard and a Freestone pavement and a garden behind it, situate in Basinghall Street ward," so writes Stow in his book on London, and that, meagre as it is, is the only description I have ever seen of the old original Hall. Stow also gives a few particulars as to the ward, which are of interest to Girdlers. "The name Basing being derived from the ancient family of Bassing, which was in this realm a name of great antiquity and renown; they were owners of the ground, one of the family was mayor 1251, and others sheriffs in 1279 and 1308." He also goes on to say that the family have now died out.

205

The Girdlers do not seem to have possessed a hall until about the year 1435, and it is probable that before that time the Company held their meetings at the great shop or selde known as Girdlerselde, mentioned before, or else borrowed the hall of some other fraternity, and this is confirmed by a note in the Brewers' records dated 1422, " The names of divers crafts and fraternities that did hire our hall during two years (1422-3), with the sums of money which they did pay." Then follows a list in which the name of the Girdlers' Company occurs.

It was not until the year 1431 that Andrew Hunt, Girdler, gave two tenements and a parcel of land, with an entrance gate under the solar of Matilda, wife of Thomas Maundevill, in the parish of St. Michael de Bassyngeshawe, to the Wardens of the Mistery of Girdlers in the City of London, and their successors, charged with the maintenance of certain tapers and observances of his obit at the church of St. Lawrence in Old Jewry, provision to be made for two poor members of the mistery who have the livery of the same, and sevenpence to be paid weekly to the poorer of the two. In case of default made in carrying out the terms of his will, the property was given in trust for sale for the good of his soul and for charitable gifts to the poor of the Mistery of Girdlers. Dated London, 24 January, A.D. 1431.

This then appears to have been the beginning of Girdlers' Hall, and this is confirmed from the Company's own records, as fortunately a book compiled by order of the Company in the year 1560 escaped the Great Fire of 1666, and is still in their possession, and gives the names of all benefactors up to that time, and what they had given to the Company. The entry as to the Hall runs as follows:

" Imprimis Andrewe Hunte in his last Testament dated the xxiiii daye of January in the year of our Lord God 1431 and in the xth year of Kyng Henry Vth Gave unto the Company Two tenements and a voyde piece of ground with the appurtenances together with a greate gate and an entrye under the solar of Maude Moundevyle these two tenements are now the Hall and the voyde grounde is the yarde at the comyng in thereof The solar of Maude Moundevyle is the chamber over the entrye and gate at the comyng into the Hall The said Andrewe Hunt by his said Testament gave the said two tenements and voide ground unto this Companye of Gurdelers and unto the Vicar of Saint Lawrence in the Old Jewry joyntly together (but as in the said will at length you maye understand that the vicar was joyned with ye Companye for no availe to hym) but his dirige money if he were at it (*i.e.*, present) as an overseer to see his will and testament to be kept

and that the said Companye of Gurdelers should
fynde for ever in the church of Saint Lawrence
within the Old Jury of London 5 tapers of wax of a
pounds weight in every taper to be burned before
the image of Saint Lawrence and to be renewed
iv tymes in the yeare and also to be kept in the
same church for ever every yeare the Sondaye
after Saynt Lawrence Daye an anniversarye with
placebo and diridge by note with ryngyng of Bells
(the Vicar to have if he were resydent xvi pence
or else nothyng vi priests iiiid apiece ii parish
clarkes iid apiece and the ryngers of ye Bells)."

The other material parts of the will have been
given above.

On this piece of land the Girdlers seem to have
erected their Hall, and in a list of Companies' halls
of the City of London reputed to be dated about
the year 1456, the hall is mentioned as standing,
but before we say anything more as to the building, the same old book goes on a little later to say,
" As for all the anniversaries and Lightes that this
Companye were bound to fynde whatsoever as
all chauntry lande anniversaries & Lightes were
gyven unto Kyng Ed. VI by Act of parliament
This Companye purchased all that we were bounde
to fynde of the same our Late Soveraigne Lord by
a Deede of Sale from hym to us by Mr Hynde
& Mr Turk Aldermen & Mr Blackwell Towne
Clerke which deede is bounde with the said evid-

ence." Stow's "London" again confirms this statement as to the purchase back from the King, because he says: "Several of the Companies having
had lands, etc., left to them for various charitable
purposes, to which was commonly added certain
rents upon those lands or tenements for the cele-
bration of their yearly obits and for priests called
chauntry priests to say mass on set days in the
churches where they were buried, for their souls
deliverance from Purgatory, and for the souls of
their particular friends and relations deceased.
Now this being a nursery of superstition and a
maintenance of idle priests, by an act of Edward VI all such gifts were granted to the Crown,
and accordingly all such lands and possessions
were seized into the King's hands, and so all such
portions of the rents of them as were appropriated
for superstitious uses were as rent charges paid
by the Companies to the King. This was a great
blow to the Corporations of London, which were
extremely weakened in their incomes and revenues,
their charities and donations being brought almost
to an end. They had no other way of putting this
right but to purchase back such rent charges and get
as good pennyworths as they could from the King.
This they did by selling other of their lands to
enable them to purchase. When they had so done
they employed the same to good uses according to
the first intent, abating the superstition.

"The Girdlers' Company purchased of the King in rent per annum, 19*s.* 2*d*.

"They sold no land. They pay to a poor de-caied brother out of this land per annum £1 10*s*."

Thus it will be seen that the Company now possess their land and Hall entirely free of any charge.

The Chronicle goes on, "Also there is in the chest a deede that no man shall buyld against our Hall wyndows in the Garden, and that our raigne water shall fall at the kytchen in the same Gardeyn without Lett of any person or persons." This garden in question was not given by Andrewe Hunt, but was the gift of a later Girdler, Robert Belgrave, in 1505, and the gift is set out in the Chronicle: "Robert Belgrave by his testament dated the 15th day of August, 1505, and in the xxth yeare of Kyng Henry VIIth gave unto this Companye (as in his Testament doth appear) a Tofte of Lande a Sollar & Garden lying within an allaye callyd Moundevyle allye late called Myddletons Allye within the said parish of St. Mychaell nowe comyng from Bassyngshawe through the said allye. The narrowe piece at the entryng in at the gardeyn dore and within the Dore nowe parcell of the gardeyn is that called the Tofte of lande and the buildyng over parte of the same now a Gallarye is the soler, and as for the Gardeyne is manyfest enough by itselff and thus is comprehendyd the whole Hall and every part of the same of many peces made one by us the said Companye." Later on, namely, in 1657, a further piece of land adjoining the Hall was purchased by a past Master, by name Roger Layton, for the sum of £200, and presented to the Company, and the Company added still further to this by the purchase of another little bit of land for £305, and thus the whole of their land in Basinghall Street was acquired.

To return to the old Chronicle for a minute a list of "Gyfts to the Hall presented by early benefactors is set out therein, and they vary from the sums of xx shillings of redy monye down to smaller sums, but many of the gifts were in kind." Thus Mystris Belgrave, the wife of Robert Belgrave, just mentioned, gave many gifts on various occasions, all sorts of things, from table-cloths, cakes of waxe weying 1^d weight, and cupps.

"Sylver" was a very favourite "gyfte," and there are many entries of presentations of this.

John Bartholomew gave to the Hall "a pott of sylver gylt, with a cover, the foote of it with a rynnyng vyne and a butterflie upon the cover," and there are several others mentioned.

In the reign of King Henry VIII a determined effort seems to have been made to furnish the kitchen, and a general "benevolence" was levied on the Company, and the list is headed.

"The Benevolence of the Mr and Wardens and all the hole clothing towards the kytchyng stuff and other thyngs in the xxx[th] year of the raigne of kyng Henry the eighth, and to remayne in the house at all tymes to be occupied as follows: John Thompson a fryeng pan, a pottell pot and a drinking pott," and then follows a whole list of articles of a like nature. Curiously enough, later on, namely in 1562, a "benevolence of the lyvery towarde the buyldyng of the kytchen and parlor" is set out, and the "some of the said Benevolence = 35.13-4." This looks as if the kitchen and parlour had then recently been burnt down, because it was curious the Company should have collected and bought the utensils so many years previously if there was no kitchen to use them in.

Glass windows were a very favourite gift about 1560, and pewter trenchers were another, but "nappkynes" were the commonest, and were nearly every year presented to the Company by some or other of the ladies of the Past Masters "of their good will."

Mysteris Wyet, widowe, and sometyme wife of Francis Hewete, gave to the Hall the 15th day of August, 1567, the parcelles hereafter following, that is to say:

"Firste, one table clothe of diaper.

"Item, one towell of diaper.

"Item, a dozen of napkynnes of diaper, all newe."

Education also was not forgotten, and the Company's library, if small, was comprehensive. It consisted of a bible and "two large chronicles, one beginninge from the first inhabitinge of England to the Conquest, and the other from the Conquest to the yeare 1586." This was further enriched a hundred years later, as "a Mr. Goodcoale, a minister, presented eight bookes to this Company of a sermon preached by him at Pawles Crosse." In return for this generosity the Court ordered inquiries to be made if he was "a man of good life and conversacon," and if so a guinea was to be presented to him.

It seems to have been customary for the Masters' wives in the sixteenth century to work something for the use of the Company during their husbands' year of office, and there are many examples of this, such as Mrs. Agnes Aheman, who gave "six lowe stooles for women, covered with greene tapestry, and fringed with greene cruell fringe, and marked on the toppe in the middle with letters embroidered T. ^{s}A., for the name of her and Mr. Thomas Aheman, her said husband." Not much beyond this is known of the old hall, except that in accordance with a precept of the Lord Mayor, "two dozen of buckets, Two long ladders, Two Hooks, Six shovels and six pickaxes," were kept in readiness there for publique use in case of fire, and in 1643 it was reported by the Court to be in a very ruinous condition, and they had no money to repair it, and in 1648 "the greatest valuation that could be made of the Hall was after the rate of £40 per annum." Of the internal decorations the following minute, dated 1629, will give some sort of an idea as to the ornamentation.

Ordered that the old table of the Queen's Arms, which stood in the Hall, and which was lately taken down, being much decaied, be refreshed, and also a table of the King's Arms made and both set in the hall, and likewise that the old table of the Arms of the several Companies of the Cittie of London, which did stand in the Garden house be new made.

The old hall was destroyed in the Great Fire of London, September, 1666. There is nothing in the minute book of the time giving any account of the burning; in fact it is hardly mentioned in the minutes beyond the fact that it was destroyed, but the account books show that 6s. 8d. was paid into the Chamber of London, "for the fee to the Surveyor to sett out the foundation of the Company's ground in St. Michael's, Bassishaw, and also the Company's own surveyor, Mr. Oliver, was paid £1 10s., for his paines in drawing out and making a modell of the ground belonging to the Company in St. Michael, Bassishaw," but this was very generally done at the time, so that people might know which was their own ground and which was their neighbours'.

In October of the same year the Court met at Leathersellers' Hall, and the first order made was that in respect of the great loss the Company have sustained by the late awful fire. " That the allowance of £6 yearly heretofore paid to Mrs. Elizabeth Taylor, late the wife of Edward Taylor, clerk of this Company, be totally foreborne and suspended," and the minute goes on "the Court now falling into serious debate and consultation concerning the heavy loss sustained by the late dreadful fire. For and what yearly resources they had left, and likewise what stock they had left, together with what debts now due and owing by the Company to any person at interest, which upon examination they found to be £800. Five hundred whereof being due and owing to Mr. Foord, and the other £300 to Mr. William Davies, the clerk, both under the seal of this Company, and being offered now by Mr. Warden Goodfellow on behalf of Mr. William Davies, that by reason of the great losses he had sustained in the late Fire, he made request that the Company would be pleased to think of some speedy way of satisfying the said £300 and what interest may be due thereupon." All which being seriously debated, several proposals were offered, and ultimately it was resolved that the goods and plate belonging to this Company and not spent should be sold for the satisfaction of the said £300, and thereupon it was proposed that Abraham Chambers, Esq., and Mr. Maximilian Bard, who had been great benefactors to the Company by their gifts of large pieces of plate, and Mr. Warden Goodfellow's own Father had given a faire piece of plate to the Company, which was yet in the stock of the Company, were asked whether they were all contented that the same plate, formerly of their gifts, should be sold with other the plate of this Company."

"They all declared their free assents, which the Court accepted from them very kindly, and thereupon it was ordered that the plate belonging to the Company, and now in their possession, should be sold to the best advantage, and the money arising therefrom should be paid to Mr. Davies towards the satisfaction of the £300 and interest, and it was likewise further ordered in case the value of the said plate should not amount to that value, then other goods as might best be spared belonging to this Company should likewise be sold, so that the said debt of £300 with the interest may be fully satisfied and discharged, and the Company's obligation be cancelled. Consideration was then taken at this Court of the distressed condition of the poor almsmen belonging to this Company inhabiting their almshouses of the foundation of George Palyn, and of the great loss the Company had sustained by the destruction of the houses in the late fire, which was for the maintenance of the said poore men. Several proposals were made for the accommodation of the said poore almsmen, the Company being very willing that some provision should be made, otherwise they must of necessity perish."

"Whereupon, after full debate, it was ordered that the sum of £20 should be paid and advanced to the poore almsmen out of the lands and stocks belonging to the Company by quarterly payment to date. And it was ordered that the ground in Sherborne and Abchurch Lane, whereon the houses formerly stood, should be employed for the maintenance of the said poore almsmen."

As a further means of raising money, eight Yeoman Girdlers and six artizans, Wireworkers and Plateworkers were called to the Livery, and the Court enforced the fine on those who were summoned and refused to accept, and shortly afterwards the fine was raised. No dinners were held for five years. Members of the Court who did not attend its meetings were fined, and a voluntary subscription was raised among the whole Company to start a fund for rebuilding, and it was further ordered that no money should be expended upon any plea whatsoever, except under the hands of three of the Committee at least.

The Company remained very quiet for the next ten years, saving all the money they could for the rebuilding of their Hall, the only act of note during this time being the purchase of a small piece of ground in the front, from a Mr. Samuel Philip and his wife, but on election day, 1680, the Master, Mr. Richard Poulton, proposed to the Company, " as worthy of their consideration, the thought of rebuilding the Hall, seing the great inconveniences that attend the Company for want of a convenient place to assemble in, and he also suggested that the longer omission of so necessary a work may be some reflection or disparagement. He therefore desired them to consult amongst themselves what may be the fittest and most suitable way to effect it, and particularly as he thought that they should consider how many persons they would think fit to be nominated by the Court of Assistants to be chosen as a committee to meet from time to time, as they should think fit, and consult with workmen, and whenever they have resolved upon anything, to report it to the next Court of Assistants for their approbation and confirmation. This was agreed to, and builders were invited to submit models and draughts, and on the 23rd September, 1680, several draughts or models were submitted, and those by Mr. Samuel Workman and Mr. Lowe were particularly approved, and thereupon the Court resolved to proceed to laying the foundation, and upon viewing the ground, it being very boggy and uncertain, Mr. Lowe proposed to bring

up the foundation even with the foreyard at £5 per
rodd, which the Court thought too much, but told
him, if he would stake and plank it well, and make
a firm and good foundation, they would give and
allow him £4 10s. per rodd, which Mr. Lowe
accepted, and promised to do the work for his own
reputation well, but the Court were to be at the
charge for the staking and planking. The Master
thereupon reported at the next Court, that upon
a further consultation about the rebuilding of the
Hall, it was the opinion of several good workmen
that the best place to put it was upon the foundation that was now laid out, and he likewise acquainted the Court that he was very well satisfied
by the said workmen that the difference between
setting the Hall upon pillars and setting it upon
the ground floor will be £300 at least in all. This
the Court were satisfied with, and were of the
same opinion, and after several minor matters had
been settled, on the 24th January, 1681, several
workmen brought in their estimates, and upon
examination of such valuations or prices, the Court
agreed that Mr. Phillips, the carpenter, was the
lowest, and thereupon the Company called in the
other workmen, and informed them that they intended to keep only with him, and discharged
them from further attendance upon that account,
and the clerk was instructed to draw up articles of
agreement with Mr. Phillips."

Once more the past Masters came forward to the help of the Company, and provided funds to assist in the rebuilding, and amongst others, Mr. James Sotherby, "an old Master," made what in these present times would be called a sporting offer; "he offered towards the rebuilding of the Hall one of three things: either to give the Company £20, or to lend them £100 under the seal of the Company, to receive for the same £10 yearly for 14 years, or to give them £100, he to have for the same an annuity of £10 per annum during his life." The Court agreed to accept the last proposal. The Master reported that old Master Wickens had handed him £100 on loan towards the rebuilding at £4 % and the clerk also lent £100 for the same purpose, for twelve months gratis.

The Company's old cash books show the prices paid for all the various parts of the building, but it is not proposed to set them out here. The contract with Mr. Phillips was for £700, but his extra charges made it up to £783. The stained window with the Company's Arms, which is still in the Hall, cost £16 10s. The old table and forms, still used, and the former probably the heaviest in London, and very clumsy, cost £60, and the total for everything, including gratuities, amounted to £1,428 4s. 10d.

On the 15th August, 1681, being election day,

the Hall was sufficiently far advanced to be used and opened; the Company does not appear to have had any particular ceremony beyond the usual election formalities, and as the then Master had taken great pains and interest in the rebuilding, he was continued in his office for another year, although he did not wish it, but, as the Company persisted, he consented to serve again. Apparently ladies were present at the dinner in the evening, and Mrs. Hickford, a Girdler's widow, on her departure, placed in the Master's hands five guineas (valued in the cash book at £5 7s. 6d.), which she freely gave towards the rebuilding of the Hall. The gift was kindly received by the Court, and the clerk ordered in future to summon and invite Mrs. Hickford to all the general feasts of the Company.

No account of the Hall would be complete without a short account of "the magic carpet," now hung up on the north wall and facing the gallery and screen (the latter, tradition says, to be by Sir Christopher Wren, although the only connection I have been able to trace between Wren and Girdlers' Hall is the fact that his godfather, Cristopher Parris, who left him a piece of gold of twenty shillings, and also the Company a dinner, was a Girdler past Master), this carpet, which has had quite a romantic history, has only within the last few years been discovered, although it lay for over two hundred years in the Company's Hall in full view, but the account, published in 1900, now slightly revised and set out later in this chapter, gives the story sufficiently fully.

The Company were evidently rather proud of their new building, and hired a soldier armed with a musket "to ward the hall." This warding did not last very long however, and in 1694 the Company took a more important step in insuring the building against fire, and the entry runs: "Paid for Insurance of the Hall from fire for the term of eleaven yeares at ye Bear bournes office by mutuall contribucon, £15 2s."

Over the entrance to the Hall is the Music Gallery, and here the Company placed a little model of their saint, who has sat up there ever since, regarding with benevolent eye the proceedings of many generations of Girdlers carried on in their Hall; and here we may take the opportunity to set out his official description, which includes the Company's armorial ensigns, as given by the Heralds' College, thus. First, then, the arms, which are per fess azure and or, a pale counter changed, three gridirons, with handles in chief of the last.

The crest. Issuing out of wreath nebuly proper a demi-figure of St. Lawrence the Deacon, crined grey and tonsured, and ensigned with a halo of gold, vested in a blue dalmatic, with amice, collar, orphreys, and fringes all of gold, and holding in dexter hand a gridiron, as in the arms, and in sinister a book of the Gospels, bound in red, with gilt leaves and clasp.

The mantlings. Ermine, double azure, powdered with clouds and sunbeams, both proper.

The badge. The figure of St. Lawrence, as in the crest, issuing out of hazel clouds, both proper.

The Heralds' College say no motto is recorded, though the motto of the Company generally accepted is, "Give thanks to God"; but I am rather inclined to think myself that this motto was not the original one but crept in somewhat later, and that the motto quoted by the Master, Mr. Edward Taylor, in his speech to the Company in 1637, " Love as Brethren and continue as friends," is the true one, especially as he had once been clerk, and, therefore, had better opportunity of being well acquainted with the Company's documents and history than other members of the Guild; but against this view must be mentioned the fact that the motto on the carpet, about the same date, is the one now used.

These arms, according to a minute of 1634, were confirmed under the hand and seal of the King of Arms, in the reign of Henry VI, about the same time as the Company's incorporation.

Lady Bateman has recently presented the Company with a copy of these armorial bearings, beautifully worked in silk, and corrected in accordance with the description given by the Heralds' College.

To return to the carpet, Robert Bell, the donor, was born in the year 1564, and was a man of gentle birth, apparently of great wealth, and one who took a leading position in the commercial life of the time. His residence at Wimbledon, known as Eagle House, and which he is stated to have built himself, still stands, and at present is the home of Mr. T. G. Jackson, R.A. In addition to his membership of the Girdlers' Company, he was also Deputy Alderman of Lyme Street, and a prominent director of the East India Company from its establishment in 1600, and is named in the Charter as one of the first " Committees."

In April, 1634, the then master of the Girdlers' Company dying in office, Mr. Robert Bell was elected Master for the residue of the year, and at the expiry of his term of office appears the following minute, 12th August, 1634.

" Also at this Court Mr. Robert Bell did present a very faire long Turkey Carpitt with the Company's Arms thereon, which he freely gave to the use of this Company as a remembrance of his Love."

The carpet, which appears from the minute books of the East India Company to have been made at the Royal Factory of Lahore, established by Akbar the Great, is of Persian design, of the so-called Gerous type, is about eight yards long and two and a half yards broad, and is knotted by hand throughout in wools of various colours, and amongst other features, has an unusually wide border. It bears in the centre the Company's arms and crest, a half-length figure of St. Lawrence holding the book of the Gospels in his right hand, and a gridiron, the emblem of his martyrdom, in his left; underneath is a scroll with the Girdlers' motto, " Give thanks to God," whilst flanked right and left Mr. Bell's arms are wrought, namely, azure, an eagle displayed, argent; in chief three fleur-de-lis or, and introduced between these and the Company's arms are two bales of merchandise, stamped with Mr. Bell's initials and trade marks. The carpet luckily escaped the Great Fire when the Hall was burnt down, from which it would almost appear that the person in charge of the Hall understood its value; but for many years past it lay on one of the Company's tables, where no one suspected its worth, until it occurred to the members of the Court, prominent among whom were the then Master, Sir Alfred J. Newton, Bart., at that time Lord Mayor, Mr. Rich, the father of the Company, and the Upper Warden, Mr. Stratten Boulnois, that its history should be inquired into. This was warmly supported by the Court, and the matter was referred to a committee for inquiry and research, and they fortunately received great assistance from Lady Bateman, the wife of Sir Alfred E. Bateman, K.C.M.G., a past Master, who recognised the arms on the carpet as identical with those displayed at Eagle House, Wimbledon, Robert Bell's old house. Communication was then made with the India Office, who looked up the old books of the East India Company, and fortunately came across the original entry of the order for the carpet and its arrival in England, at the disposal of the said Robert Bell, and so conclusively established its identity. The Court then, on the recommendation of Mr. Ernest Normand, asked the advice of Mr. St. John Hope, of the Royal Society of Antiquaries, and Sir Caspar Purdon Clarke, C.I.E., of the Victoria and Albert Museum, South Kensington. These gentlemen placed their services at the disposal of the Company, and advised that the carpet should be cleaned, repaired, and framed, and finally the matter was left in the hands of Sir C. Purdon Clarke, who had it removed to the Museum, where he could personally superintend the cleaning and restoring. There the ink spots were removed and the rents repaired by the Decorative Needlework Society, and the carpet returned to the Hall, and subsequently framed in a large oak frame, carved by Miss B. Campbell, a former pupil at the South Kensington Museum, in a style to correspond to the present mouldings of the Hall, and also with this inscription: " The Gift of Robert Bell, Master, A.D. 1634, in remembrance of his love," and finally Sir Caspar Purdon Clarke came down and added to his other great services the task of getting the carpet in its frame and fixed to the wall; and the Company, in honour of the occasion, gave a lunch to the India Office, when Lord George Hamilton, Sir George Birdwood, and many other distinguished guests were invited, and came and examined the carpet, which is of its kind, probably unique in the City of London, and outside the Victoria and Albert Museum has very few rivals in England.

Now that the carpet has been discovered and exposed to view, people from all parts of the world have come to see it, and prints and coloured designs have been made and circulated in many of the art museums and schools of Europe, and recently Lord Curzon has presented a large coloured print of it to the museum in Calcutta, so that its fame and beauty is gradually penetrating even as far away as its original home.

The Company, having rebuilt their Hall, set about beautifying it, and all sorts of devices were resorted to, the arms of many of the past Masters were set up in the windows, and the names of the Company's benefactors inscribed on the walls, and many presents of small but necessary articles, such as carpets, table-cloths, and such like things were made to the Company, so that they soon acquired a regular stock again; this was carried so far, that in 1690 Mr. Ryley, the King's painter, asked to be excused serving the office of steward, and offered to present the Company with the King's picture at large, very well done; this the Court accepted, it being esteemed an additional ornament to the Hall. After two years, however, Mr. Ryley asked to be exempt, on the payment of £15 instead, and to this the Court unfortunately agreed.

On the east side of the Hall is the Court-room, in ruder times called the Women's Parlour, and afterwards the Ladies' Parlour, and which was begun at the same time as the Hall, but enlarged in 1735; this room is panelled and also enriched with some handsome carving, and in particular possesses some beautiful Grinling Gibbons carving, which has been painted over by a former member of the Company; this room is lighted by three windows, one of which has painted on it an old sundial, with the motto, *tempus omnia minat*.[1]

The Court-room walls are hung with old plans of various lands and houses, left to the Company by members of the Guild, also with a set of Hogarth's engravings of the Idle and Industrious Apprentice, presented by Dr. Laidlaw Purves, a

---

[1] Probably *tempus omnia terminat*, but the "*ter*" has been lost.

past Master, and a medal, with six clasps, in commemoration of the Boer War, presented to the
Company by the War Office, in recognition of the
efforts of the Company on that occasion. Over the
fireplace, too, a picture of an Italian scene is inserted in the panelling ; this was presented in
1860 by Robert Smiley, a past Master, and the
picture, it is stated, was painted by his wife, but
experts have thrown doubt on this, and rather un-
gallantly have said it is too well done for an
amateur. This room looks out on the garden, with
its mulberry tree, which still bears a good crop
every year, and the off-shoot of an old fig-tree, the
parent stem of which was blown down a few years
ago, and which it is believed had been growing for
over 150 years.

In former times the Garden must have been of
far greater extent than at present, and probably
included the land on which the Company has built
several houses. The old account books give a fee
of 4s. 6d. for cutting the grass several times in
every year, and the Company was always laying
down dozens of gooseberry bushes, rose trees, and
also currant bushes, though it is doubtful if many
gooseberries reached the mouths of the past Masters, as the children were allowed to play in the
garden, and no doubt looked upon the fruit as part
of their privileges. The City had evidently fewer
smuts flying about than at present, as we read that

on certain occasions "the Company's washing and napery was hung up to dry in a corner of the garden, which would be quite out of the question in these days.

The new Hall being opened, and the Company still being very hard put to for funds, the building, or various parts of it, was let out for all sorts of purposes, such as for the use of the Sheriffs, also for dancing classes, religious meetings, and mathematical lectures; the latter tenancy having a clause that the past Masters should be allowed to attend the lectures free of charge.

The present ornamentation of the Hall is very simple, consisting of the screen at the end, and some Grinling Gibbons carving; there are also half-a-dozen banners, presented, according to custom, by Masters who have held the office of Lord Mayor, and also two silk banners, beautifully embroidered with silk and gold thread, the work of Miss Marion Humphry, of Crowborough, and presented by a past Master, Mr. C. H. Silverside, these latter banners representing the City and the Company's arms respectively. There is also a large picture attributed to Carracci, of Eli Blessing the Infant Samuel, presented in 1870 by Mr. William Cobbett, afterwards a member of the Court, which is hung immediately over the fireplace.

In recent times the Company has added a drawing-room adjoining the Gallery of the Hall, and the stranger entering here catches sight of a very curious cabinet, painted with the arms and heraldic devices of all the states of Europe, with their various orders of nobility and knighthood; this is a unique thing, and was painted and presented to the Company by the late Mr. G. W. Rich when Father of the Company; some of the figures are extraordinary small, and what is more astonishing is that the work was not commenced until Mr. Rich was well over seventy, and was finished in his eightieth year.

This room was built in the year 1878, during the Mastership of the late Mr. John Potter, and at the same time the Company rebuilt the offices and kitchen, and a stone was set up, giving the names the Master and Wardens that year, the name of the architect, Mr. Woodthorpe, and the builders, Messrs. Ashby and Horner.

In 1837 the Company determined to thoroughly renovate and do up the Hall which had fallen somewhat out of repair, and over £1,000 was spent in putting the place into a thorough state of repair, and in making various improvements.

The Company possesses one other picture, a landscape, after the style of Constable, and painted by Mr. Chester, and presented to the Company by his widow in 1900, representing a scene on the Wey, outside Guildford. Unfortunately, owing to lack of space, this picture, which in its day was hung on the line at the Academy, is not very well placed, but it is so large that it is not an easy thing to put it in a spot where it can be seen to advantage. A very few words are necessary to give an idea of the Company's plate, which, although at one time before King Charles' day was of considerable value, yet, as we have seen after those strenuous times, came down to nothing,[1] and so remained until about eighty years ago, when Mr. Eddison, a past Master, presented a handsome rose-water bowl; this was followed shortly after by a cup, presented by Mr. Goodall, a member of the Livery, and another presented by Mr. John Planner. In the last few years Mr. T. V. Bowater has given another cup, and Mr. J. A. Skinner a handsome pair of silver candelabra, which latter are always placed before the Master on occasions of State dinners, but as will be seen from the above list, the Company is by no means rich in plate, and cannot make anything like the show that some of the smaller Companies can do in this respect.

This then is Girdlers' Hall as it stands at present, and although it is not very large, it is, when viewed at night, well lit up, with the old carpet at one end, the screen at the other, and its hanging banners, justly esteemed one of the most comfortable, and at the same time, handsome looking halls in the City of London.

[1] The Company possesses an old silver cup, dated about 1666, the gift of Mr. John Wickens, twice Master of the Company.— W. D. S.

CAP. IX

CHARITY

As he pronounces lastly on each deed
Of so much fame in heaven expect thy meed.
Lycidas.

THE consideration of the Charities of the Girdlers' Company falls naturally under two heads, those where the Company act as Trustees and Administrators under some will or scheme settled by the Court of Chancery and Charity Commissioners, and those which flow from the Company's own bounty out of their own moneys, and the latter may vary from a donation towards the rebuilding of a church steeple " to the enlargement of a window," as will presently more fully appear.

Perhaps the simplest plan would be to take the settled schemes first, and deal with the miscellaneous afterwards, and before we proceed to discuss the various characteristics of the former there is one curious point that should be noted, and that is that nearly all the Company's larger charities

233

were founded during the reign of Queen Elizabeth, or within a few years of her death, apparently during that golden period of our history; men of all classes and grades had not only learned to think Imperially, but also to act so, and the greatness of the times was not confined to poets and statesmen, but spread into all the various walks of life, and so it was with the members of the Girdlers' Company, and although unfortunately the minute books for the greater part of this particular period are missing, we can gather from the names which have come down and from the charities that were founded then and still exist, that the Company, too, had its giants in those days, and we are reaping the benefits of their munificence at the present time.

One of the most important of our Charities founded then was that of Mr. Cuthbert Beeston who, by his will in 1580, bequeathed a certain messuage in Southwark, known as the Cage, and seven other tenements there to the Master and Wardens of the Company for ever, subject to the life interest of his wife, Alice, upon certain trusts, which showed that he took a wide and comprehensive view of things, and understood the necessity for both spiritual and material matters.

First of all 40s. was to be delivered to the Livery on the day of his burial for a drinkynge or recreation to be had and made amongst them; further,

£4 was to be given for ever to the relief of the stewards, to be expended by them towards the amendment of the quarterly dinners, also for ten years after the death of his wife four sermons were to be preached each year in the Church of St. Stephen, Coleman Street, the preacher of each sermon to receive the sum of 5s., but should the Gospel not be sincerely preached in the same parish during the ten years, then the £1 per annum was to be distributed amongst the poor of the said parish instead. In these days, when every one's rendering of the sincere preaching of the Gospel differs from his neighbour's, this latter bequest would be a somewhat delicate question to handle, and there seem to be the ingredients of a first-rate Chancery action involved in this bequest.

The Master and Wardens were also enjoined to distribute amongst the poorest inhabitants of the said parish every year two cartloads of great coals, one load before the Feast of All Saints, and the other on or before the Feast of our Lord God. The Clerk and the Beadle were also not forgotten, and the sum of twelve pence apiece was to be paid to them for their trouble in distributing the same. The remainder of the rents to remain in stock to be lent freely to the poorest men of the Company (they giving surety for the same), for the term of one year free of interest, and so to continue for ever. This was carried out for about 250 years, until 1824, when the estate was required for the purpose of widening the approaches to the New London Bridge; and accordingly the land was sold, and the money realized from the sale was invested in stocks. The next year the Charity Commissioners and the Company came to the conclusion that the original intentions of Mr. Beeston were now impracticable, and a scheme was drawn up and sanctioned by the Court of Chancery for the building and endowment of almshouses for the reception and maintenance of aged and decayed free brothers of the Company and their widows, but care was taken to preserve the small payments to the Stewards and the Clerk, etc., in accordance with the terms of the original will.

Accordingly, in pursuance of the agreement, seven almshouses were built at Peckham, and have ever since been inhabited and filled, in accordance with the scheme, by poor free brothers of the Company,[1] and in one instance, in 1847, a late member of the Court "being decaied in his estate" was elected to one of the houses. The houses have a pleasant piece of green in front with some fine trees, and each of them has a nice sized garden at the back, where in summer time the

[1] One of the almsfolk, Miss Martin by name, at present (1904) inhabiting the houses, remembers coming with her father, who took great interest in the buildings, and inspecting the houses before they were finished.—W. D. S.

aged folk can amuse themselves by tending their flowers, and some of them take great pride and interest in the cultivation of their little plots of land. These almsfolk are periodically visited by the Master and Wardens and members of the Court, and the Clerk also regularly visits them on quarter days for the purpose of paying the pensions, and until recently they used to come to the Hall after the Livery dinners for the broken meats and a bottle of Pensioners' port, and on these occasions the Master and Wardens were accustomed to don large white aprons and assist in cutting up the different joints and dividing the various delicacies, but even in the City old customs have a tendency somehow to drop out, and this one has recently disappeared, although the almsfolk are otherwise compensated. Twice a year also they each receive a small extra sum for coals, the gift of a pious benefactor, Richard Mountford, who in 1833 left the interest on £400 Consols to be distributed amongst the poor of the Company as the Court should direct, and so the money was given to these almsfolk, and is a very welcome addition to their pensions. Free from care and worries, and with the knowledge that whatever happens they are always sure of their pension, most of them live to a great age, and there is an instance preserved in the minutes of a letter written to the Court by a son of one of the almsfolk, thanking them for their kindness to his father for many years past, and informing them that his father had passed "quietly and soberly away" at the age of 103.

The next Charity is that of Mr. George Palyn, another Girdler, who in 1609 gave to the Company by will £900, and directed that they should within two years after his death, with £260, part thereof, obtain a permission from the King under the great seal of England, authorizing the Company to erect a hospital or almshouse in or near the City of London, for the perpetual relief and sustentation of six poor men, and to endow the same with lands and hereditaments, and should build an almshouse or hospital to contain at least six rooms, wherein six aged, blind, or impotent men might severally dwell, and that they should within three years after his decease with £640 residue of the said £900 purchase in the Corporate name of the Company, lands, hereditaments, and tenements, in fee simple of the clear annual value of £40 at least, towards the maintenance of the six men, being of honest repute and Freemen of London, that is to say, to each of them yearly £6 13s. 4d., by quarterly payments.

Letters patent for the above purpose were granted to the Company in April, 1612, and next month the Company purchased a plot of ground in the Parish of St. Giles, without Cripplegate, now St. Luke's, Old Street, and erected thereon a hospital or almshouse, containing six separate dwellings. The Company also purchased freehold premises, as an endowment for the almshouses, and at the Company's own expense it was ordered that a Bible and service book of a large print, together with a desk to lay the same on, should be bought, to remain in the hospital or almshouse for the use of the almsmen therein.

These almshouses were destroyed by fire in 1666, as were also the houses bought by the Company in Sherborne and Abchurch Lanes, and whose rents went for the maintenance of the said poor almsmen, and in consequence they were put upon half pay, and even this the Company had to provide from their own funds.

The houses were rebuilt in the course of time at a spot going by the exhilarating name of Pest-house Row, and they were again rebuilt in 1745, but a little more than a 100 years later, namely, in 1849, the Committee reported that the almshouses were too dilapidated to repair, and advised their removal, and the same time they informed the Court that one of their members, Mr. Thomas Watkins, had most generously offered to give the Company a piece of land at Peckham, as a site for new almshouses on Palyn's foundation. This was accepted, and the cordial thanks of the Court were accorded to Mr. Watkins for his munificent gift, and shortly after new houses were built on the land presented, and the almsfolk removed there at the Company's expense, and Mr. Watkins added to his former kindness by providing them with a very good dinner that day, and the Court on the same evening provided him with a dinner, and a copy of the resolution of the cordial thanks of the Court, inscribed on vellum, and signed by the members of the Court, was presented to Mr. Watkins in appreciation of his munificent gift.

The Charity and the almsmen benefited greatly by this gift, as the Company were able to let the piece of land at Bath Street, on which the old almshouses stood, out on building lease, and the revenue derived from this was used in augmenting the pensions of the almsfolk and in increasing the general usefulness of the Charity.

This Charity, like Beeston's, has also gone through the refining fire of the Court of Chancery, and is now administered in accordance with a scheme, confirmed by the Charity Commissioners, by which a certain amount of the surplus income goes in pensions, and also a certain amount in support of hospitals and other institutions for the relief of poor persons residing in London or its vicinity.

On the foundation of both sets of almshouses the Court drew up a set of rules to be observed by the inmates, and any serious breach of them was punishable by expulsion, though the Court were very loth to put this remedy in force. Some of the misdemeanours of the almsmen read rather quaintly in these times, such as " harbouring children," "reviling and quarrelling of wives about drying of clothes," " neglecting prayers," "swearing and other incivilities," the latter being a vice to which an almsman of the name of " Benjamin Love " was particularly apt at, but managed to escape with " a mulct."

These houses are situated near those of Mr. Cuthbert Beeston, and are managed and administered much on the same lines, and the almsmen are fortunate each in the possession of his own little garden, which it is no exaggeration to say is a source of the greatest pleasure and pride to them, and the writer well remembers the complaint of one of the old almswomen, nearly eighty years of age, who moaned about her illnesses, not so much for the discomfort it caused her, but because it prevented her attending to her garden and so she was afraid the others would get ahead of her.

At both sets of houses the Company assist the almsfolk to keep the front gardens bright and tidy by having a gardener in to do the heavy work once a week.

The next Charity is that of Richard Andrews, and is known in the Company as Andrews Charity.

This was founded in quite a different way from the others, and was the outcome of the fact that in 1637 Richard Andrews was chosen Master of the Company, and "being now present, he did intimate to the Court that, in respect to his great weakness and debility of body, he should be compelled to reside in the country and be very much absent, and thereby less able to perform the duties of the office of Master of the Company which was required, and therefore did desire the Court to allow him to be excused the position of Master, and he would not only take it as a great courtesy done unto him but would also submit to such fine as the Court should think fit with great willingness and thankfulness. Now forasmuch as the Court did verily believe that the said Richard Andrews did not through waywardness or unwillingness desire to be excused and free from the said office of Master for the reasons before expressed, and also that at a prior Court in August, 1631, he being then elected Renter Warden, did not only fine for the office of Master whenever it should happen (although the Court did not assent thereto), and for his then exemption did give to this Company the sum of £100 to be employed for the first three years for the benefit of the Company, and afterwards to be bestowed on the purchase of a piece of land of as great value as could be bought therewith, the yearly profit thereof to be bestowed amongst the poor of this Company as the gift of the said Richard Andrews, and that also the Company having lately found a convenient purchase, but of greater value by fourscore pounds, the said Richard Andrews, on being made acquainted with the same, did voluntarily bestow and give the aforesaid fourscore pounds more for attaining the said purchase, with the desire that the Court would be pleased in respect thereof to free him from the said place of Master of the Company. It was ordered that the said Richard Andrews should be exempted from bearing the said office of Master of the Company."

This then was the foundation of Andrews Charity, and to this day it is distributed quarterly in the form of pensions amongst a certain number of the poor of the Company in accordance with Mr. Andrews' wish, and they are known as Andrews' Pensioners, and the Company possess the original cash book opened when the Charity was first instituted, which accounts are most clearly written and kept and show how the money has been distributed amongst the poor of the Company without a break down to the present time.

A very favourite form of charity in Queen Elizabeth's reign was the bequeathing of sums of money by wealthy members of the Company to be lent out free of interest to poor young freemen just out of their apprenticeship, to give them a start in life. The Company had no less than six small sums, varying from £20 to £50, left them by pious Girdlers for this purpose alone between the years 1577 and 1603, and the immense service they rendered to young freemen is strikingly set out by the following minute in 1632: "Mrs. Richard Chambers gave £50 to be lent out for ever to poor young men of the Company, free of interest and upon such security as the Master and Wardens should approve of or without security, as a thankful remembrance of God's great blessing to her late husband, Mr. Richard Chambers, deceased, who from the like stock of money which he had lent to him to begin the world with much increased the same by God's blessing upon his endeavours."

All these small moneys were unfortunately lost at the time of the Fire of London, and when the Charity Commissioners in 1830 made inquiry as to them, the Court returned answer stating that prior to the Great Fire the money had been duly applied agreeably to the directions of the donors. That all the bonds taken for the repayment of the then existing loans having been destroyed in that fire, an order was made by the Court held 24th June, 1667, that the Clerk should make out the best account in his power of such advances, but as no entry appears of his having been able to do so, or of the repayment of such sums then lent out, the Court consider that the moneys given by these various benefactors were lost to the Company.

The repair of highways and bridges, which in olden times was left more to private efforts rather than public bodies, was another favourite form for pious benefactors to exercise their charity, and one of the earliest Girdler charities we know of was in connection with this duty, and in 1447 John Costyn, citizen and girdler, bequeathed to his wife certain property for life, charged with observing his obit with silent mass of one of the five joys of the glorious Mother of God, and further with the distribution between the vigil of All Saints and Easter Eve so long as his said wife shall live of 100 quarters of coal among the poor of the parish, a single man or woman receiving weekly one bucket of good measure, "full be heped," with an ultimate remainder under certain circumstances to the Vicar of the Church of St. Lawrence in the Jewry and the Wardens of the Mistery of Girdlers of the City for the time being in trust for sale, the proceeds to be devoted to the repair of bridges and highways, the bestowal of marriage portions, and other pious and charitable uses.

A " baker's dozen " is an expression sometimes heard, and the will of Henry Flycke, in 1559, is an official recognition of this custom, as he bequeathed a house or inn, called by the sign of

" The George," at Hammersmith, to the Company
on conditions, they to give every Sunday for ever
after the day of his burial to thirteen poor people
of the parish of St. Bride in London one dozen
of bread, accounting thirteen to the dozen, also
100 faggots to the poor of the same parish. This
bequest was literally carried out by the Company
for nearly three hundred years, when the Court of
Chancery made an order that £50 per annum
be rendered instead; and some time after that, at
the instance of the Charity Commissioners, the
annual payment was redeemed. The Company
still possesses the account book of this charity,
starting from its initiation and showing the payments regularly made until its redemption.

The Company possess other land at Hammersmith in addition to the George Inn, and in
former days the piece of land was a strawberry
garden, and every now and again the Master and
Wardens were accustomed to drive down to Hammersmith " to take a view of the Company's property there." On these occasions the tenant seems
to have provided a strawberry feast, and the Court
in return made an order that the tenant and his
daughter should be asked to dinner on Election
Day next, and they also thoughtfully included his
granddaughter in the invitation, but the granddaughter and the strawberries have vanished long
since, over one hundred and fifty years ago in

fact, and the only fruit grown at Hammersmith now, or at any rate on the Company's property, is more in the nature of that which is known as ground rent.

Coming down to more modern times, early in the last century, two small charities were founded by Mr. Welch and Mr. Paynter for poor widows under certain circumstances, and a little later, namely, in 1850, Mr. Alderman Sidney, who was also Lord Mayor of London, gave a sum of money to be funded, the dividends arising therefrom to be given to deserving decayed members of the Court, and when there was no applicant the same to be reinvested as an Augmentation Fund.

The Company is also the fountain head of certain other charities, such as that founded by Mr. Thomas Nevitt in 1633, who gave a piece of land in Romney Marsh, Kent, the rents and profits thereof to belong to the Girdlers' Company to pay certain small sums annually to various parishes in different parts of England; but this is not of sufficient interest to set out beyond the fact that the sums are annually rendered, and the Clerk also receives the sum of 4*d*. per annum under another small charity of the like nature,[1] which sum the accounts show conclusively is never forgotten, but is annually drawn by that official, and a small sum given by the testator to the poor of St. Bride,

---

[1] Founded by Mr. George Davison in 1541.

Fleet Street, on the anniversary of his death, is annually rendered.

Turning now to miscellaneous charity the distribution of which is paid out of the Company's own funds, apparently their charity was not confined to any particular branch or channel, and appeals of every conceivable kind were and are regularly submitted, and nothing seems to come amiss, indeed, I think it is no exaggeration to say that the old time minutes show at every Court application for relief and assistance under some set of circumstances or other, which applications were promptly answered by the Company so far as their means would admit, and according as they thought the petition deserving, and not only in cases of actual necessity, but also in many other ways where assistance could be properly granted, and a favourite form was in the help of education, of which there are many examples like the following: "1622. John Ware, a poore free brother, petitioned the Court for money to assist his sonne at the University; the Court continued his pension of £3 in respect that the said Ware was an honest poore man and his child very hopefull." This carries us back to the days when many of the boys at the Universities lived in extreme poverty, sometimes even having to beg their bread, so that £3 was a matter of some moment to a poor scholar.

Widows, too, had a large claim on the sympathy

of the Court, and the following somewhat quaintly worded entry is typical; the entry is also interesting as showing the harshness of the law in the seventeenth century:

"Widdowe Madox alleged that she had been cast into prison for want, whereupon it was ordered that if she could be discharged out of prison for 40/ or under, that the same should be paid for her enlargement." Evidently this was sufficient, as the cash book shows " To so much paid for the enlargement of Widdowe Madox 40/."

Assisting poor maids on their marriages was another favourite form of benevolence on the part of the Company, so in 1629, "upon the request of Edward Taylor, Clerke of this Company, it was ordered that the sum of 40/ shal be given unto a poore maid servant of his towards her marriage."

Religion and the assistance of poor ministers played a large part in the Company's charity, especially in the days of the Puritans, and I fear that the Court was sometimes rather humbugged, as the reply was generally favourable "if the Master and Wardens upon speech with him found that his conversation was godly," but perhaps the Company, although willing to assist, occasionally did so with their tongue in their cheek, as the following rather hints at: "Also at this Court upon the humble petition of Luccius Fressa an Italian schoole M^a who had as he alleged left his country and was minded to live in this kingdom in respect of the purity and truth of the religion here professed. It was ordered & agreed the rather for that he brought letters testimonial under the hand of Mr. O. Nettleford of his honest and religious life & conversation that the some of 40/ should be given him as a benevolence out of the house stock towards his reliefe."

The Company distributed much money in connection with the Plague, not only in London, but also sending to the relief of other towns, such as Bury St. Edmunds, "on the occasion of their being afflicted with the sad contagion £5," and I believe a small chapel in one of the churches in that town is named the Girdlers' Chapel out of gratitude for this assistance, and the same occurs at Coventry, but for what reason is not known.

Later on we find the press gang at work, and the Company assisting various goodwives, being distracted on the sad occasion of their husbands being taken by the press gang.

These few examples will give some idea of the various channels in which the Company's bounty formerly flowed, and, of course, at this present day the Court is always assisting some individual in temporary or permanent distress, either by means of donations or pensions, or assisting in making up some fund to the required amount so as to enable some undertaking to be carried out, such as the donation they gave in 1884 during the Mastership of Mr. T. W. Weeding to enable the Vicar of St. Michael's, Coventry, to claim a large sum promised to rebuild the steeple of the church, and also repair the building, although, as a general rule, their charities are more confined to the district lying in and around the Metropolis.

Many institutions, too, founded for the relief of the poor and the helping of the sick, are annually subscribed to, and the claims of education are not forgotten, and amongst the latest schemes in respect to the latter may be mentioned the foundation of a small scholarship at the Guildhall School of Music, and the initiation, during the recent Mastership of Dr. W. Laidlaw Purves, of a Girdlers' Lectureship in Economics at Cambridge University, but this latter is at present only tentative, and has not been irrevocably agreed upon by the Court, who have to use great discrimination in the distribution of the funds at their disposal, as the number and various nature of the claims are so great, and it is no exaggeration to say that on an average about six different sorts of appeals for votes or money on behalf of some person or institution arrive at the hall every day, so that the Court has a very wide and ever-increasing field in which to exercise and distribute the flow of the Company's funds to charity or otherwise, but so far as the funds of the Company will afford, these appeals are always carefully considered and responded to.

Such then is the history of The Worshipful Company of Girdlers so far as I have been able to put it together, and although, perhaps, it cannot be said that we have made any very great noise in the world, or that our deeds are sufficiently noteworthy to be written " in letters all of gold," still I cannot help thinking that it was from the efforts of small guilds and fraternities like this, with the constant and unremitting care of our forefathers in office to preserve the standard of the article manufactured, and " to remedy the abuses of these times," that English workmanship attained, and perhaps still holds, the premier place in the opinion of the world for thoroughness and efficiency, and that in itself is no light thing, and therefore, although owing to the change of fashion, and the decay of the trade, our usefulness in this respect has somewhat died out, yet we can still point with satisfaction to the administration of our charities, and the distribution of our bounty with the numerous institutions benefited and individuals assisted and encouraged, so that we still drink with pride in Girdlers' Hall the ancient toast "The Worshipful Company of Girdlers, Root and Branch, and may it flourish for ever."

APPENDIX

LIST OF MASTERS OF THE COMPANY

1180 RALPH DE LA BARRE.

1209 PROBABLY GERARD THE GIRDLER.

1216 BENET LE SEINTURER, SHERIFF OF LONDON.

1328 RALPH DE BRAGHYNGE.

1329 JOHN POTYN.

1333 JOHN DE PRESTONE, MAYOR OF LONDON.

1344 RICHARD WAYTE.

1354 JOHN ABRAHAM.

1371 THOMAS CHARLEWODE.

1417 JOHN NASYNG.

1420 JOHN HENET (*circa*).

1444 JOHN COSTYN.

1500 ROBERT BELGRAVE (Master two or three times).

1528 G. W. DAVISON.

1539 JOHN THOMPSON.

1551 HENRY FLYCKE.

1553 LAWRENCE ROBIANT.

1560 FRANCIS HEWETE.

1562 HENRY BUCKFOLD.

1566 —— WRIGHT.

1567 JOHN GRAYE.

1570 CUTHBERT BEESTON.

1571 WILLIAM BRIGHTE.

1573 THOMAS MUSSETT.

1581 RICHARD CHAMBERS.

1595 GEO. PALYN (*circa*).

253

1598   Sir Stephen Soames.

1600   Thomas Aheman.

1617   Thomas Nevitt.

1618   Brown.

1621   John Auburg.

1622   Humphry Brown.

1623   Humphrey Lyall.

1624   Arthur Lee.

1625   Robert Greene.

1626   Samuel Watts.

1627   John Lambleton.

1628   Thomas Stead.

1629   Randall Wetwood.

1630   Robert Davies.

1631   Richard Chambers, Jun.

1632   Thomas Barrow.

1633   Thomas Baggolly, died in office.

1634   Robert Bell, elected in April for the remainder of the year.

1635   Samuel Davies.

1636   Anthony Huson.

1637   Edward Taylor.

1638   Edward Taylor, 2nd year.

1639   Joseph Tylden.

1640   Matthew Pariss.

1641   Roger Heyton.

1642   Thomas Marsh.

1643   Christopher Punchon.

1644   Abraham Chambers.

1645   Abraham Chambers (Alderman, elected 2nd time).

1646   Roger Heyton, 2nd time.

1647   William Hodgson.

1648 OLIVER CLUEBERRIN.
1649 ABRAHAM CHAMBERS, 3rd time.
1650 ALDERMAN C. TWINCH.
1651 LEONARD LOBELL.
1652 MAXIMILIAN BARD.
1653 JOHN CROSBIE.
1654 SAMUEL LEE.
1655 RICHARD HORTON.
1656 RICHARD LLOYD.
1657 THOMAS ALLEN.
1658 GEORGE GILBERT.
1659 ABRAHAM CHAMBERS, 4th time.
1660 JOHN TAYLOR.
1661 THOMAS RUSKE.
1662 THOMAS BOSTOCKE.
1663 MAXIMILIAN BARD, 2nd time.
1664 ROBERT DAWKES.
1665 JOHN WICKENS.
1666 GEORGE DAY.
1667 JAMES SOTHEBY.
1668 JOHN CUDWORTH.
1669 MATTHIAS GOODFELLOW.
1670 JOHN WEBB.
1671 ISAAC RUTTON.
1672 JOSHUA LASHER.
1673 ROBERT VIDOR, unable to serve.
1673 JOHN WICKENS, shortly afterwards chosen, 2nd time.
1674 ROBERT PORTER.
1675 THOMAS GODSON.
1676 CHRISTOPHER FLOWER.
1677 JOHN MORGER.
1678 DANIEL BLUNDEN.

1679   CALEB GROSVENOR, served half the year.
1680   RICHARD POULTON.
1681   RICHARD POULTON, 2nd time.
1682   JABEZ JEFFRIES.
1683   SAMUEL WINGE.
1684   JOSEPH SCRIVEN.
1685   SIMON SMYTHE.
1686   SIMON SMYTHE, 2nd time.
1687   EDWARD NOURSE, chosen Master, but removed
       by order of the King, and THOMAS WOODMAN
       elected in his stead.
1688   EDWARD NOURSE, 2nd time.
1689   ROBERT SEXTON.
1690   ROBERT TAYLOR.
1691   EDWARD LORDS.
1692   WILLIAM BARD.
1693   RICHARD CHAMBERS.
1694   MARMADUKE BLUDDEN.
1695   EDWARD ROOKE.
1696   JOHN TAYLOR.
1697   WILLIAM HEYWOOD.
1698   EDMOND CLARKE.
1699   DANIEL COLEY.
1700   WILLIAM COOLING.
1701   WILLIAM COOLING, 2nd time.
1702   THOMAS SMITH.
1703   ROBERT PETER.
1704   EDMOND CLARKE.
1705   EDMOND CLARKE, 2nd time.
1706   DANIEL OLEY.
1707   BAZIL LAMB.
1708   JOHN HARRIS.
1709   JOSEPH SANDWELL.

1710 WILLIAM SHADDOCK.

1711 ROBERT SHRIBB.

1712   DRAFTGATE.

1713 JOSEPH BILLOW.

1714 RICHARD DRAPER.

1715 CHARLES SMITH.

1716 JAMES CANE.

1717 JOHN POLLARD.

1718 FRANCIS GARTHORNE.

1719 JOHN BENNY.

1720 ZACKARY GISBOURNE.

1721 JOHN EYRES, died during year of office, and JOHN OLEY was elected in February, 1722, for the remainder of the year.

1722 CAMBELL CHASE.

1723 PETER CROSS.

1724 THOMAS THORPE.

1725 JOHN PETCHE.

1726 SAMUEL WHITFIELD.

1727 JOHN BOSVILLE.

1728 DANIEL GARRETT.

1729 THOMAS SMITH.

1730 EDWARD SMITH.

1731 WILLIAM BENSON.

1732 PETER CROSS, 2nd time.

1733 WILLIAM BRIGHT.

1734 JOHN GOODFELLOW.

1735 HENRY TROLLOPE.

1736 THOMAS RHODES.

1737 WILLIAM POWELL.

1738 HENRY DOBSON.

1739 RICHARD SHERGOLD.

1740 FREDERICK DRAFTGATE.

1741 ADAM BARLOW.
1742 CHARLES GORING.
1743 MICHAEL HATTON.
1744 JOSEPH OAKES.
1745 WILLIAM CRIPPS.
1746 EDWARD WALDO.
1747 WILLIAM NIGHTINGALE.
1748 SAMUEL ROOD.
1749 WILLIAM MATTHEWS.
1750 ; SAMUEL BOWTERS.
1751 JOHN FFAWCETT.
1752 BENJAMIN SMITH.
1753 JOHN PEGOU.
1754 WILLIAM LORD.
1755 TIPPING BUSTAT.
1756 JAMES HARRISON.
1757 JOHN SYMONDS.
1758 WILLIAM JORDAN.
1759 MARK STONE.
1760 JOHN BATTIN.
1761 JOHN WARD.
1762 CYRUS MAIGRE.
1763 WILLIAM POWELL.
1764 JAMES CHALOTT.
1765 JOHN ALPHONSUS COSTE.
1766 EDWARD WALDO
1767 RICHARD HOPE.
1768 THOMAS COX.
1769 THOMAS SPARSHOTT.
1770 EDWARD WALDO, 2nd time.
1771 EDWARD WALDO, 3rd time.
1772 JOHN WARD.
1773 WILLIAM ELYETT.

1774 JAMES COLES.

1775 CYRUS MAIGRE, 2nd time.

1776 JOSEPH WELCH.

1777 JOSEPH KILBY, died during year of office, THOMAS COX elected for remainder of the year.

1778 JOHN TOPLIS.

1779 RICHARD HOPE, 2nd time.

1780 JOHN ADOLPHUS L'OSTE.

1781 JOSEPH EDWARDS.

1782 SAMUEL THORNE.

1783 JOHN SHERER.

1784 JOSEPH SMITH.

1785 JAMES CHAPMAN.

1786 CHARLES SINCLAIR.

1787 GEORGE HAIGH.

1788 JOHN PATY.

1789 JOHN HEALEY.

1790 SAMUEL WAIGHT.

1791 JOSEPH WELCH, 2nd time.

1792 WILLIAM MOBBS.

1793 JAMES COLE, died during year of office, and JOSEPH WELCH elected for the remainder of the year, 3rd time.

1794 WILLIAM CALVERT.

1795 FENTON ROBINSON.

1796 GEORGE BLACK.

1797 WILLIAM ELLIZETT.

1798 WILLIAM SABINE.

1799 JOHN CARRUTHERS.

1800 DAVID SEWELL.

1801 JAMES ELISHA.

1802 EDWARD GULLARD.

1803 CHARLES L'OSTE.
1804 JOHN BARBER.
1805 JOHN BLAKE.
1806 WILLIAM HOWARD.
1807 MORGAN GOULD.
1808 THOMAS CATO.
1809 ROBERT MAWBY.
1810 JOSEPH MADDOX.
1811 RICHARD MOUNTFORD.
1812 JOHN WEST, subsequently
     JOHN ANDERSON.
1813 JOSEPH WELCH.
1814 BENJAMIN HOWARD.
1815 JESSE CATO.
1816 JOHN HAMMON.
1817 JOHN SHERER.
1818 SAMUEL PAYNTER.
1819 JOHN WOODHOUSE.
1820 JOSEPH BONSER.
1821 JAMES JENKINS.
1822 JOHN GARFORD.
1823 WILLIAM ALLEN.
1824 ROBERT ANDERSON.
1825 JOHN TAYLOR.
1826 JOHN EDDISON.
1827 FRANCIS GRAHAM.
1828 FREDERICK COOLEY CHAPPEL.
1829 GEORGE SMITH.
1830 SAMUEL THOMAS COLEMAN.
1831 WILLIAM MORGAN.
1832 THOMAS BAKER.
1833 JOSIAH CATO.
1834 FREDERICK THOMAS WEST.

1835 WILLIAM CORY.
1836 THOMAS WATKINS.
1837 GEORGE BAKER.
1838 EDWARD HALSE.
1839 LOUIS MICHAEL SIMON.
1840 SAMUEL WHITE SWEET.
1841 WILLIAM WESTALL.
1842 THOMAS HAYTER LONGDEN.
1843 CHARLES MARTYR.
1844 WILLIAM EDWARD EDDISON.
1845 HENRY ROBERT BRIGGS.
1846 EDWARD PETER HALSE.
1847 GEORGE KNIGHT SMITH.
1848 WILLIAM ROBERT SMILEY.
1849 ALDERMAN THOMAS SIDNEY.
1850 JAMES ELAND HOBSON.
1851 JOHN HULBERT.
1852 JOHN HULBERT, 2nd time.
1853 HENRY LAMB.
1854 HENRY LAMB, 2nd time.
1855 JOHN JERRAM.
1856 CHARLES WILLIAM STOKES.
1857 WILLIAM MOUL.
1858 WILLIAM CORY, JUN.
1859 THE RT. HON. DAVID WILLIAM WIRE, LORD
       MAYOR.
1860 THOMAS BAKER.
1861 RICHARD WESTALL.
1862 JOHN BAGGALLAY.
1863 LOVELL AUGUSTUS REEVE.
1864 HENRY BRIGGS.
1865 CHARLES ANDERSON DIXEY.
1866 WILLIAM MORLEY WESTALL.

1867 GEORGE WILLIAM RICH.
1868 GEORGE WILLIAM RICH, 2nd time.
1869 GEORGE DAVISON GIBBES.
1870 JOHN ARTHUR BUCKLEY.
1871 GEORGE EDWARD PHILBRICK.
1872 THOMAS MORRISON FAIRCLOUGH.
1873 BENJAMIN FOX WATKINS.
1874 JOHN EDWARD SIMMONS.
1875 JOHN JOSEPH POWELL, Q.C.
1876 GEORGE ARTHUR GADSDEN.
1877 JOHN POTTER.
1878 FREDERICK ADOLPHUS PHILBRICK, Q.C.
1879 FREDERICK ADOLPHUS PHILBRICK, Q.C., 2nd time.
1880 GEORGE WILLIAM RICH, JUN.
1881 JOHN CRIDDLE.
1882 MORRISON FAIRCLOUGH.
1883 JAMES DALTON.
1884 THOMAS WEEDING WEEDING.
1885 THOMAS WEEDING WEEDING, 2nd time.
1886 ALFRED EDMUND BATEMAN.
1887 JOHN ARTHUR BUCKLEY, 2nd time.
1888 JOHN EDWARD SIMMONS, 2nd time.
1889 JAMES TURNER.
1890 EDWARD COFFIN.
1891 WILLIAM COBBETT.
1892 JOHN BRIDGMAN GAPP.
1893 HARRY BECK.
1894 CHARLES HICKES SILVERSIDE.
1895 FRANK FAIRCLOUGH.
1896 FREDERICK WILLIAM NELSON LLOYD.
1897 FREDERICK WILLIAM NELSON LLOYD, 2nd time.

1898 ALDERMAN ALFRED JAMES NEWTON.
1899 THE RT. HON. SIR ALFRED JAMES NEWTON BART., LORD MAYOR, 2nd time.
1900 STRATTEN BOULNOIS.
1901 WILLIAM JOSEPH DOWNES.
1902 WILLIAM LAIDLAW PURVES, M.D.
1903 SIR FREDERICK DIXON DIXON-HARTLAND, BART., M.P.
1904 JAMES HARMER DALTON.

TRADE ORDINANCES OF THE GIRDLERS' COMPANY.

Item. It is ordered Ordeyned and Established that for the preventing and avoyding of all deceipts abuses and defects in the makeing and working of all the wares and workes belonging to the Art or Mistery of a Girdler or the keeping vending or putting to sale of any such bad or defective wares that his M^{aties} liege people may not be deceived in the buying thereof No p̄son or p̄sons Freeman or Forreyners Aliens or Denizens that now doe or doth or hereafter shall use or exercise the said Art or Mistery of a Girdler or anything thereto appteyning as Trimers Guilders Buckle Makers Harnesse makers and all other artificers to the said Art or Mistery belonging and which now doe or hereafter shall inhabit within the Citty of London Libtyes and suburbs thereof and three miles compasse of the same Citty shall make any Girdle or Belt with any other harnesse or buckles than such as shall be made within this Realme or the dominions thereof or shall garnish any Girdle belt or garter with any other

metall than cleane metall of Gold Silver lattin [1] iron or
steale And the Buckles thereof shall be truly and sub-
stantially made with chapes of iron or of good thick plate
and that as well all chapes plates and buckles of all
Girdles and belts whatsoever shall be firmely riveted with
two rivetts att the least as allso all strapps and side
pieces of Belts shall be firmely riveted to the Hanger
neither shall any leather wherein there is a flaw or cutt
or any sheepskin be wrought upp or goe to the makeing
or lineing of any Girdle belt or bandileers nor any leather
to be wrought or used therein shall be worse than calves'
skin well tanned and dressed Neither shall any Collars
for bandileers be made of any worse stuffe or matter then
good neate's leather well tanned and dressed and not to
be lesse then two inches in breadth Neither shall any
Girdle Belt garter or bandyleer or any p̄t or p̄cell of
them be wrought or stitched with any copp lace or thread
or with copp mixed with silver Neither shall any vallure
or counterfeet velvet or other counterfeit stuffe be used
or wrought upp in any Girdles belts garters or bandyleers
or shall be guilded damasked or sangunid in any worse
manner than in the ensamples from time to time to be
showed and p̄duced to them at the Hall of the said Company by the Master & Wardens for the time being on
paine that all and every p̄son aforesaid that shall offend
in any point of this present ordinance contrary to the
true meaneing thereof or shall have or keep in his or their
Shopp or Shopps Workhouses or Warehouses any such
bad insufficient or deceiptfull goods or wares with in-
tenc̃on to vend or put the same to sale shall forfit and
pay unto the Master and Wardˢ or Keep̄ˢ of the Art or

---

[1] Lattin means, according to some authorities, iron tinned
over.

Mistery of Girdlers London for the time being to the use of the same Company the full worth and vallue of every such Girdle belt Garter and Bandileer as the same shall be vallued by two other p̄sons of the s^d Art and Mistery and also all and every such Girdle or Girdles Belt or Belts Garter or Garters or Bandyleers shall be seized by the said Master and Wardens or any one of them and carryed to the Hall of the s^d Corporac̃on to the end the same may be defaced or otherwise so disposed of as to the Master Wardens and Assist^{ts} or the Major part of them assembled in a Court of Assistants in their discretions shall think fitt every of which said forfeitures to be in default of paym̄t thereof recovered or leavyed in such maner as is hereinafter appointed

Item. It is ordered ordeyned and Established that for the preventing of all fraudes in the makeing and working of all the wares belonging to the said Art or Mistery of a wireworker or Plateworkers that His Mãties subjeĉts may not be deceived in the buying thereof all and every p̄son & p̄sons as well Freemen as Forreyners and all others that now do or which hereafter shall use or exercise the said Art or Mistery or anything thereto appteyneing within London the Libtyes thereof or three miles compasse of ye same Citty shall make and worke all wyer workes and plate works of good substantiall and lawfull wyer & plate and shall make them only of such sorts and kinds of wyer and plate as are fitt for the severall uses and workes and as of right they ought and of none other and in the makeing of all hookes and eyes they and every of them shall platt the hookes before and crosse the eyes and make them of good and sufficient wyer and that noe thows and black auletts shall be made of fyne wyer but of coarse fyne wyer and shall be well made and platted

and that all wyer that shall be made into Buckles as well
revying wyer as other shall be well joyned and tongued
with bastard wyer hard and well filed and that all stock
cards wool cards and all other wyer cards whatsoever shall
be truely and sufficiently made and wrought with good
and substantiall wyer in calves' leather and not in sheeps'
leather and that as well all maner of fish hookes needles
and all sort of chains cages window wyers sives trapps
and all other wyerworkes whatsoever as also Lanthorns
dripping pannes and all maner of plateworks whatsoever
and all other thinges belonging to the said Art or Mistery
shall be sufficiently made and wrought of good substantiall and lawfull matter and stuffe on paine that every
p̄son that shall offend in any point of this present ordinance or shall have or keep any such bad or deceiptful
wares in his or their shopp or shopps Workhouses or
Warehouses with intenc̄on to vend or expose the same
to sale contrary to the true meaneing hereof shall forfit
and pay to the Master and Wardens or Keeps of the Art
or Mistery of Girdlers London for the time being to the
use of the same society the full vallue of all and every
such bad and deceiptfull wares and workes as the same
shall be vallued by two other p̄sons of the same Art and
Mistery and also all such bad and insufficient wares shall
by the s^d Master & Wardens for the time being or any
one of them be seized and carried to the Publique Hall
of the s^d Company to the end the same may be defaced
or otherwise so disposed of as to the s^d Master Wardens
and Assistants or to the Major p̄t of them assembled in
a Court of Assistants in their discretions shall be thought
meet every of which said forfeitures to be in default of
payment thereof recovered or leavyed in such manner as
is hereinafter appointed

266

Item. It is Ordered Ordeyned and Established that no p̄son or p̄sons free of the s^d Society shall at any time or times hereafter pack or put up any goods wares or workes belonging to the s^d Arts or Mist^{ryes} or either of them for sale at any Faire or Market before such time as the same Goods shall be shewed unto or viewed by the Master & Wardens or one of them to the intent that they may foresee that the same be substantiall lawfull and sufficient wares for sale and it is furth^r Ordered and Ordeyned that no Freeman or the Servant of any freeman of the said Society shall at any time or times hereafter go a hawkeing or p̄ffer their Goods to Sale in the Streets from Shopp to Shopp or in any Inn or other place or places within London or Libtyes thereof or three miles compasse of the same Citty unlesse it be to another free brother of the said Company upon paine that every p̄son that shall offend against any part of this p̄rsent ordinance shall forfeit and pay to the Master & Wardens or Keeps of the Art or Mistery of Girdlers London for the time being to the use of the said Society the sume of thirteen shillings fower pence of lawfull money of England for ev^ry such offence to be in default of payment thereof recovered or leavyed in such manner as is hereinafter appointed.[1]

---

[1] A later Ordinance says that these fynes are to be recovered by aceon of Debt or accon of the Case in any of his Māties Courts of Record or alternatively to leavy the same by distresse of the Goods and Chattels of the p̃son chargeable.

ADDENDA.

EXTRACT, DATED 1575, FROM AN OLD MEMORANDUM BOOK OF THE COMPANY.

Mr. Cuthbert Beeston Master of the said Company of Girdlers the said yere, of his owne free will gave unto the use of the M^r of the said Companye yerely to be elected, & chosen for ever, one crowne Garlande of black velvett, imbrodered with the lres of his name, a Toune and a gredyron of golde and the girdle wth the buckles of brodered gold lace compassynge the crowne of the said garland.

LIST OF THE MASTER, WARDENS, ASSIST-ANTS AND LIVERY OF THE WORSHIP-FUL COMPANY OF GIRDLERS.

4TH AUGUST, 1904.

Master.

MR. JAMES HARMER DALTON.

Wardens.

MR. HENRY PULBROOK.
MR. HENRY HICKS.
MR. EDWARD SIMMONS.

Assistants.

MR. GEORGE WILLIAM RICH.
HIS HONOUR JUDGE FREDK. A. PHILBRICK, K.C.
MR. GEORGE WILLIAM RICH, JUNR.
MR. MORRISON FAIRCLOUGH.
MR. THOMAS WEEDING WEEDING.
SIR ALFRED EDMUND BATEMAN, K.C.M.G.
MR. JAMES TURNER.
MR. HARRY BECK.
MR. CHARLES HICKES SILVERSIDE.
MR. FRANK FAIRCLOUGH.
SIR ALFRED JAMES NEWTON, BT.
MR. STRATTEN BOULNOIS.
MR. WILLIAM JOSEPH DOWNES.
DR. WILLIAM LAIDLAW PURVES.
SIR FREDERICK DIXON DIXON-HARTLAND, BT., M.P.

THE WORSHIPFUL COMPANY

Mr. Thomas Potter.

Mr. William Joynson-Hicks.

Mr. George William Barber.

Livery.

Mr. William Hollis Luce.

Mr. David Rose.

Mr. William Saunders.

Mr. William Cobbett.

Mr. Thomas Fredc. Smith.

Mr. James William Butler.

Mr. Simpson Whistler.

Mr. Arthur Jerram.

Mr. William Richard Baggallay.

Mr. Walter Fairclough.

Mr. William Charles Lynne.

Mr. Alfred Lindsey Buzzard.

Mr. William Thomas Dayton.

Mr. Joshua Jones.

Mr. Arthur Fairclough.

Mr. William Hewson Lees.

Mr. William Downie McCombie

Mr. William Homer.

Mr. James Henry Mitchiner.

Mr. Richard Rhod Swann.

Mr. Reginald St. Aubyn Roumieu.

Mr. Percy Fairclough.

Mr. William Cowland.

Mr. William Manuel Potter.

Mr. Harry Butler.

Mr. Thomas Stafford Sidney.

Mr. Frank Moul.

Mr. Sidney Herbert Terry.

MR. WILLIAM CRASTER PHEASANT.
MR. JOHN MATHISON FRASER.
MR. LEWIS POTTER.
MR. ROBERT ALEXANDER BRIGGS.
MR. EUSTACE SHERRARD.
MR. LESTER JOHN TERRY.
MR. NORMAN FREDERICK HARRISSON.
MR. JOHN EDWARD LAYTON.
MR. JOHN KEELINGE BATEMAN.
MR. WILLIAM DUMVILLE SMYTHE.
MR. HARRY HOTTINGHAM NEWTON.
MR. ROBERT HALIBURTON ADIE.
MR. HENRY RICHARD WESTALL.
MR. BURRELL PAGE.
MR. ALFRED ALGERNON ROBINSON.
MR. RICHARD FREDERICK TAYLOR.
MR. CHARLES LEDGER HORNBY.
MR. GEORGE BRIGGS.
MR. JOHN HERBERT BISHOP.
MR. FRANK EBENEZER BISHOP.
MR. JAMES ARTHUR SKINNER.
MR. ALFRED ROBERT ORTON GERY.
MR. GEORGE EDWARDS.
MR. REGINALD WILLIAM JAMES.
MR. THOMAS BINGHAM MARSHALL.
MR. PERCY BRODIE ROWE.
MR. HUGH PILGRIM SIMPSON.
MR. GEORGE WALTER LLOYD.
SIR CASPAR PURDON-CLARKE, C.I.E.
MR. GEORGE PAUL ERNEST.
MR. GEORGE GRIFFIN.
MR. WILLIAM BRIGGS, M.A., LL.D.
MR. THOMAS VANSITTART BOWATER.

WORSHIPFUL COMPANY OF GIRDLERS

Mr. Alfred Allistone.

Mr. Vivian Francis Crowther Smith.

Mr. James Aylward Game.

Mr. Arthur Lambert Marlow.

Mr. Thomas Luce.

Mr. Augustus Langham Christie.

Mr. Alec Raven Briggs.

Mr. Walter Sibbald Adie, I.C.S.

INDEX

AARON'S Girdle, 8.
Abbey, Edwin A., R.A., 4.
Abchurch Lane, 217, 239.
Absolon, "the joly clerke," 75.
Adulterine Guilds, 30.
Affidavit of steward, 122.
Aheman, Mrs. Thomas, 213.
Akbar the Great, 225.
Alderman, custom as to, 109.
Almsfolk: long lives of, 237.
  on half pay, 239.
Almshouses: Beeston's, 236.
  Palyn's, 239.
Almsman: becomes beadle, 145.
  fining of, 193, 241.
"Anabasis," Xenophon's, 8.
Ancient Britons, Girdles of, 9.
Ancient Member, The, 113.
Andrews, Richard, 241.
  foundation of charity, 243.
  speech of, 242.
Anglo-Saxon Girdles, 9.
Answer to Common Council, 189.

Antiquarian Society, 44.
Antiquity, 21.
Apology to Court, 105.
Apprentice, 133.
  binding of, 133.
  complaint of, 136.
  fees on binding, 134.
  left by will, 133.
  letters as to, 135.
  made free, 138.
  numbers bound, 134, 194.
  numbers of, 134.
  ordinances as to, 133.
  punishment of, 136.
  runaway, 135.
  turned over, 136.
Aprons, 158.
Apthorpe, John, 134.
Arbalasters, 177.
Armourer's fee, 197.
Arms, Company's, 22, 222.
Artificers, 80.
Artizans, 79.
  and Attorney-General, 92, 96.
  annual meeting of, 138.

INDEX

Artizans: apologize to Court, 100.
appeal to King, 91, 96.
ask for copies, 98.
charter as to, 42.
consulted by Court, 88.
decline of, 102.
fined, 87.
number of, in 1620, 80.
petition King Edward IV, 80.
Pinners, 75.
propositions by, 95.
quarrel among themselves, 97.
summon Master and Wardens, 88.
wireworkers, 76.
Ashby and Horner, 231.
Assistants: Court of, 116.
fined for bad work, 87.
how originated, 116.
Athelstane, laws of King, 24.
Attendance at church, 162.

Badge Master, 112.
Wardens, 112.
Baker's dozen, 245.
Ball, 165.
abolished, 166.
Bandyleers, 6, 59.
Bankrupts, Girdles of, 18.
Banners, 171, 230.
Bard, Maximilian, 216.
Barge, 167.

Barre, Ralph de la, 39.
Bartholomew, John, 211.
Baselards, 12.
Basing, 205.
Bateman, Lady, 222, 226.
Bath, knights of the, 166.
Bath Street property, 240.
Beadle, 145.
almsman, 145.
compensation to, 145
gratuity to, 145.
Past Master, 145.
put on the clothing, 146.
salary of, 145.
staff of, 146.
Beeston, Cuthbert, 120, 234, 268.
almshouses, 236.
gifts to steward, 235.
scheme, 236.
Belgrave, Robert, 210.
Bell, Robert, 114, 223.
Benet le Seinturer, 32, 113.
Benevolences, 178.
Berwick-on-Tweed, siege of, 177.
Bill of fare, 152.
Bills of adventure, 182.
Binding apprentices, 134.
Birdwood, Sir George, 227.
Black Girdle, 13.
Blue Girdle, 13.
Boer war medal, 229.
Bokelers, The, 59.
Bonds, 243.

INDEX

Bonds: burnt, 244.
clerks, 143.
Renter Wardens, 115.
Bonjohn's case, 67.
Books tied to girdles, 16.
Boulnois, Stratten, 225.
Brace girdles, 60.
Bradele, Geoffrey de, 38.
Brangewayn, William, will of, 12.
Brass forbidden, 93.
Breakfast at Hall, 151, 167.
Brewers' Company, 132, 206.
Bridewell boys, 135.
Brigerdler, definition of, 36, 59.
Broad Saxon girdles, 10.
Broken meats, 237.
Bucklers, 59.
Bucks: as a fine, 108.
given, 162.
Burial from Hall, 151, 160.
Bury St. Edmunds, 250.
Butler's "Lives of the Saints," 23.

Cabinet, Mr. Rich's, 231.
Caddis girdles, 92.
Calendar of State Papers, 50.
Wills, 14.
Call to Livery, 125.
Canterbury Pilgrims, 93.
Canting Heraldry, 22.
Carpet, 221.

Carracci's picture, 230.
Carraway seeds, 159.
Cauntebrigg, John de, 178.
Ceynturer, 29.
Chambers, Abraham, plate of, 216.
Chambers, Mrs. Richard, 244.
Charities, 233.
Charity Commissioners, 236, 240.
Charles II, restoration of, 170.
Charter, 42.
of Charles I, 51.
confirmation of, 44.
cost of first, 44.
of Elizabeth, 48.
first, 41.
of James, 11, 51.
kept at bank, 45.
of Philip and Mary, 48.
surrender of, 53.
translation of, 42.
Chaucer's "Canterbury Tales," 12, 75, 93.
"Romance of the Rose," 13.
Chauntry priests, 209.
Chimney tax, 198.
Chinese custom as to girdles, 20.
Choice of livery, 124.
Chronicle Girdlers, 207.
Church service, when originated, 26.
Church steeple, repair of, 251.
"Cingulum deponere" custom, 18.

275

INDEX

City: Charter, 27.
  walls, 178.
Clarke, Sir Casper Purdon, C.I.E., 226.
Clerk, 140.
  acts as Renter Warden, 141.
  acts without salary, 146.
  becomes Past Master, 144.
  bond of, 145.
  complaints as to dancing, 141.
  dishes for, 144, 153.
  duties of, 143, 192.
  election of, 142.
  expulsion of, 142.
  fining of, 143.
  lends the Company money, 196, 220.
  losses at fire, 215.
  Past Master, becomes, 144.
  reversion to clerkship, 141.
  robs Company, 143.
  salary of, in 1790, 143.
  saves Company's goods, 140.
Clifford, William, 122.
Clipt guineas, 200.
Closheneys, 62.
Clothworkers paid by girdles, 18.
Coal provision, 179, 235, 245.
Cobbett, Mr. William, 230.
Commissions, Royal, 201.
Committee, constitution of, 113.
Commonwealth, arms of, 167.

Company: branches of, 58.
  carver, 146.
  colours, 8.
  constitution of, 103.
  father of, 113.
  fined, 177.
  foundation of, 21.
  motto, 97, 223.
  precedence of, 33
  seal, ancient, 45.
  sequestrated, 190.
  title of, 34.
Complaint of Pinners, 50.
Constitution of company, 103.
Cook, 157.
  censure of, 157.
  fining of, 157.
Cord girdles, 15.
Corn duty, 179.
Corporal punishment, 134.
Corslets given, 108.
Cost of rebuilding Hall, 220.
Costyn, John, 245.
Court, 116.
  appeal to Lord Mayor, 90.
  consult artizans, 88.
  fees, origin of, 119.
  how originated, 26, 116.
  lend money, 186.
  magisterial powers, 118.
  ordinance as to, 120.
  petition to, 136.
  removal from, 116.
  removed by King, 117.
  room, 228.

INDEX

Court: summoned, 96.
   take counsel's opinion, 92.
Cowley, William, trial of, 136.
Crown, description of, 268.
Crowning of Master, 163.
Cudworth, John, 110.
Curfew, 35.
Curriers' Company, 72.
Cutpurse, 3.
Cyclops, 7.
Cyrus, 7.

Dancing, 230.
   complaints of, 141.
Darius, girdle of, 7.
David and Jonathan, 8.
Davies, Richard, clerk, 140, 216.
Davison's charity, 247.
Death of Master, 224.
"Decaied Livery," 193.
Decay of Livery, 129.
Declaration by Liveryman, 130.
   by Master, 106.
   by Wardens, 106.
Definition of Girdler, 3.
Delivery of surrender, 55.
Delphic oracle, 7.
Derby, Earl of, 203.
Dessert, 159.
De wreches girdle, 13.
Dickens, Walter, behaviour of, 89.
Dickinson's complaint, 84.
Dinners abandoned, 217.

Dinners, behaviour at, 154.
Dishes for clerk, 153.
Disputes as to the ladies, 152.
Divident, prosecution of, 197.
Drawing-room, 230.
Drayton, Thomas, 136.
Dryncking, 160, 234.
Duties: of clerk, 143, 192.
   of Master, 71.
   of Renter Warden, 115.
   of whifflers, 139.

Earl's girdle, 12, 69.
East India Company, 226.
Economics lecture, 251.
Education, 248.
Edward III, King, joins guild, 40.
Edward IV, confirms charter, 45.
Edward VII, his girdle, 17.
Edwards, Jonadab, 117.
Election: of clerk, 142.
   day, 162.
   of first Master, 47.
   of Master, 106.
   of Wardens, 106.
Elijah the Tishbite, girdle of, 8.
Elizabeth's, Queen, charter, 48.
Ellis, Richard, speech of, 108.
Encouragement of Yeomanry, 139.
Enlargement of widow, 249.
Esquires' girdles, 11.

Ettes, William, 160.

"Euphues his England," 15.

Evelyn, John, his "Diary," 171.

Everard, Allen, will of, 13.

Exchequer Rolls, 30.

Exodus, 8.

Expulsion: of clerk, 142.
    of Renter Warden, 115.

Eyre, Geoffrey, letter of, 107.

Fabian's "Life of William Rufus," 10.

Faggots given, 246.

Fairclough, Morrison, badges of, 112.

Fairholt's "Costume in England," 9.

Faithorne's map, 150.

Father of the Company, 113.

Fees: court, origin of, 119.
    to Company's carver, 146.
    to officers, 196.

Fig tree, 229.

Financial, 176.

Fine: for Master, 109.
    for not serving, 116.
    of bucks, 108.
    of Guild, 30.
    of steward, 124.

Finley, Ralph, declaration of, 85.

Fire of London, 214.

First ordinances, 62.

Fishmongers' Saint, 22.

Flaskets of strawings, 157.

Flycke, Henry, 245.

Forraigne pynnes, 75.

"Formalities all," 169, 173.

Fortifying Derry, 184.

Foundation of Company, 21.

Freedom of apprentice, 138.

Free loans, 243.

Free woman, 128.

French girdles imported, 92.

Fressa, Lucius, 249.

Funerals, 160.

Fynes for enrolling, 135.

Gallery to Hall, 222.

Garden, 229.

Garetters, 6, 59, 60, 68.

Garters, 6, 59, 60.
    long, 16.

General Court, 162.

"George Inn," the, 246.

Gerard le Seinturer, 31.

Gibbons, Grinling, 228.

Gift: for translation, 132.
    to stewards, 170, 235.

Gilbert, George, complaint of, 118.

Girdle: ancient British, 9.
    ancient custom as to, 18.
    Anglo-Saxon, 10.
    bankrupts', 18.
    black, 13.
    blue, 13.
    caddis, 92.
    cord, 15.

INDEX

Girdle: deprivation of, 39.
de wreches, 13.
earl's, of gold, 12, 69.
esquire's, 11.
French, 92.
Georgian, 17.
inscribed with text, 13.
King Edward VII, 17.
King Henry V, 15.
King Henry VI, 14.
knight's, 11.
leather, 16.
left by will, 12.
linen, 8.
metal, 15.
Norman, 10.
Persian custom as to, 20.
Plantagenet, 11.
price of, temp. Ed. III, 74.
priest's, 10, 12.
refused for King, 86.
rope, 10.
sackcloth, 18.
scallopes, 12.
seizure of silk, 13.
silver, 14, 67.
Stuart, 16.
theft of, 19.
Tudor, 15.
two kinds of, 2.
velvet, 15.
white in China, 20.
white thread, 18.
yellow, 13.
Girdler: chapel, 250.

Girdler: chronicle, 207.
definition of, 3.
different names for, 29.
dish, 156.
first reference to, 29.
mainpernors, 36.
mayor, 113.
sheriff, 113.
Girdler's toast, 252.
Girdling, 57.
Girdlersselde, 78, 206.
Girdlestead, meaning of, 14.
Glass windows, 212, 220.
Goodcoale's sermon, 213.
Goodfellow, Warden, 216.
Goodwives' pensions, 196.
Gooseberry bushes, 229.
Gowns: how trimmed, 119, 151.
livery, 130.
Granary, Company's, 181.
Grand accompt, 182, 192, 201.
Grate cupps, 159.
Gratuity to beadle, 145.
Griddle, 22.
Grievances, petition of, 90.
Guild: derivation of word, 20.
fining of, 30.
first called Livery Companies, 40.
how originated, 25.
religious character of, 22.
St. Lawrence, 22.
Guildhall School, 251.
Gunpowder stored, 199.

INDEX

Gyfts to Hall, 211.

Haigh, G., 112.
Half-pay, 239.
Hall: 205.
  ancient valuation of, 190, 214.
  breakfast at, 151, 167.
  burial from, 151, 160.
  cost of rebuilding, 220.
  destruction of, 214.
  insurance of, 222.
  let for dancing, 230.
  let for religion, 230.
  opening of new, 220.
  ruinous condition of, 189, 214.
  Stow's description of, 205.
Hallam's history, 31.
Hamilton, Lord George, 227.
Harleian manuscripts, 10.
Harnessing and garnishing, 5.
Hearth tax, 198.
Henry II amerces guild, 30.
Henry IV confirms charter, 45.
Henry V, girdle of, 15.
Henry VI, girdle of, 14.
Herbert's history, 182.
Herodotus, 7.
Hickford, Leonard, speech of, 98.
Hickford, Mrs., 221.
Highways, repair of, 245.
Hogarth engravings, 228.

Holegh, John de, will of, 12.
Holt, Edward, 136.
Holy Graal, 104.
Homer's "Odyssey," 7.
Hooks and eyes, 77.
Hooliganism, temp. Edward I, 34.
Hope, St. John, 226.
Horn, Nicholas, 178.
Horsman, translation of, 132.
Hospitality, 148.
Household cavalry, 60.
Hume's " History," 9.
Humphry, Miss Marion, 230.
Hunte, Andrew, 206.
Hypocras, 159.

Illiterate Renter Warden, 116.
Incorporation: date of, 46.
  of Pinners and Wireworkers, 48.
Inspeximus Charter, 45.
Insurance of Hall, 222.
Ireland, plantation of, 183.
Irish estates, forfeiture of, 185.
Isley, imprisonment of, 127.
Istar, the goddess, 7.

James II, King, charter of, 51.
Jefferson, Symon, imprisoned, 104.
Jenkins, Philip, behaviour of, 89.
Jeremiah, 8.

INDEX

Jessop, Augustus, 10.
Joanna, trousseau of, 75.
John de Holegh, will of, 12.
John, King, 31.
Joint committee, 94.
Jones, John, 116.
Judge Jeffreys, 56.

Kedleston, Lord Curzon of, 227.
Keelmen of Newcastle, 33.
Kempfer, 20.
King's painter, 228.
King removes Master, 110.
Kitchen furnished, 212.
Kite, admittance of, 130.
Knights' girdles, 11.
Knight Templars, badge of, 18.

Ladies: at dinner, 152.
  power of, 166.
Lady barbers, 40.
Lanthorn makers, 77.
Layton, Roger, 211.
Leather girdle, 16.
Leathersellers' Hall, 215.
Lecturer, Girdler's, 251.
Leggy, Thomas, letter of, 66, 135.
Leviticus, 8.
Libel, release for, 119.
Library in 1586, 213.
Licence, trading without, 27.
Linen girdle, 8.

List of Masters, 253.
Livery, 124.
  bargain for, 129.
  choice of, 125.
  Company's, first called, 40.
  compulsory attendance, 217.
  decaied, 193.
  decay of, 129.
  election of, 125.
  gowns of, 130.
  notice of call to, 125.
  number of, in 1666, 124.
  removal from, 127.
  summoned wholesale, 126.
Liveryman, 124.
  declaration by, 130.
  degradation of, 128.
  imprisoned, 127.
Loan: by clerk, 196, 220.
  by Master, 173.
Long garters, 16.
Lord Mayor: letter from, 161.
  rates Master, 167.
Lord Mayor's day, 167.
Lord Protector, 170.
Loving cup custom, 155.
Low, Mr., 218.
Loyal London, 191.
Lyly's "Euphues his England," 15.
Lycurgus, 18.

Madox, widdowe, 249.

INDEX

Magisterial powers of Court, 118.

Malmesbury, William of, 155.

Malvolio, 60.

Mark, worth of, 31.

Marriage benevolence, 249.

Martyrdom of St. Lawrence, 23.

Master, 104.
  arms put up, 113.
  arms taken down, 113.
  badge of, 112.
  by proxy, 109.
  complaint of, 108.
  crowning of, 106, 163.
  declaration by, 106.
  dies in office, 224.
  dons an apron, 237.
  duties of, 71.
  duty of searching, 107.
  election of first, 47.
  fines for office, 108.
  fine for not serving, 109.
  first, 30.
  first called, 104.
  insult to, 105.
  King orders removal of, 110.
  lends money to Company, 173.
  list of, 253.
  method of election of, 106.
  pays fine not to serve office, 108.
  qualification for, 106.
  rated by Lord Mayor, 167.

Master: refused vote of thanks, 112.
  Simon Smythe, his speech, 56.

Maundevylle alley, 206.

"Mayd Emelyn, Book of," 29.

Maynard, Christopher, 121.

Meeting of the Company, 162.

Members rated, 188.

Metal girdles, 15.

Middleton, Hugh, 195.

"Miller's Tale," 75.

Ministers assisted, 249.

Misdemeanours of almsmen, 241.

Money: borrowed on seal, 185.
  lost, 244.
  raised from Livery, 186.

Moore, 21.

Moses, 8.

Mothers-in-Law, 133.

Motto, Company's, 97, 223.

Mountford's gift, 237.

Mulberry tree, 229.

Mulct of almsman, 183.

Musicians, 163.

Mystery, definitions of, 58.

Names presented, 188.

Neglect of clerk, 142.

Nevitt's charity, 247.

New London Bridge, 236.

New River Company, 195.

Newton, Sir Alfred J., Bart. 225.

INDEX

New Work, 13.
Nineveh sculptures, 7.
Norman girdles, 10.
Northwick's "History," 180.
Northy, Richard, plea of, 133.
Nourse, Ed., removed, 110.
Nosegaie, 157.
Nutmegs, 159.

Objection to serve office, 108.
Office, refusal to serve, 109.
Offspring Brown, 145.
Ogilby's, John, map, 150.
Ongham, John, 14.
Opening new Hall, 220.
Ordinances: as to apprentice, 133.
  church, 27.
  clerk, 141.
  Court, 120.
  date of first, 61.
  date of new, 89.
  trade, 263.
Original charity cash book, 243.
Orphan tax, 135.
Oysters and sausages suspended, 156.

Palgrave, Sir Francis, 202.
Palyn, Geo., 238.
Palyn's scheme, 238.
Parris, Christopher, 160, 221.

Past Master, 113.
  becomes beadle, 145.
  becomes clerk, 144.
Patent, first, 41.
Patron Saint, 22.
Patterns exhibited in Hall, 87.
Payment by girdles, 18.
Paynter's charity, 247.
Pellipar estate, 184.
Pemberton, Sir Francis, 101.
Penance, 40.
Pennebrigg, Sir Fulke, 3
Pensions to widdowes, 196.
Pepys's "Diary," 16, 191.
Perquisites of clerk, 144.
Persian: Girdler minister, 20.
  Queens, 8.
Pesthouse Row, 239.
Peter the Soldier, 200.
Petition: against translation, 132.
  by artizan, 81, 91, 96.
  of Court, 189.
  of grievances, 90.
  to Charles II, 52.
Pewter, 156.
Philbrick, Geo. E., 144.
Philbrick's, Judge, badge, 112.
Philip and Mary, Charter of, 48.
Phillips the Carpenter, 219.
Phoenicians introduce Girdles, 9.
Piers Plowman, 12.
Pikes and Muskets, 199.

283

INDEX

Pin-money, 75.

Pinners, 74.

  artizan, 75.

  dissevered by Charles I, 51.

  incorporated with Company, 48.

  joined to Company, 47.

Pins, 74.

Pipes bursting, 199.

Placing of ladies, 152.

Plague, 160.

Plantagenet girdles, 11.

Plantation of Ireland, 182.

Plate, 232.

  sold, 185, 187, 216.

  Workers, 74, 76.

Poor Law, 195.

Pope St. Sixtus, 23.

Porter, staff of, 146.

Potter, John, 231.

Poulton, Richard, 218.

Power of guilds, 41.

Precedence of Company, 32.

Precept from Lord Mayor, 161.

Present Charter, 51.

Prestone, John de, 32, 113.

Priests' girdles, 10, 12.

Progress, Royal, 170.

Proverbs, 9.

Punishment of apprentice, 136.

Purves, Dr. W. L., 228, 251.

Qualification of Master, 106.

Quaint artizans, 97.

Quarterage, 193.

  in Saxon times, 25.

Queen Mary's laws as to girdles, 15.

Queen's arms, 214.

Quest of Enquiry, 201.

Quorum, 119.

Quo Warranto, Writ of, 51.

Radishes, 159, 201.

Ralph de la Barre, 30.

Rating of Company, 189.

Raven, Andrew, 136.

  complaint against, 118.

Rearwan, Robert, acknowledgment by, 85.

Rebuilding: Almshouses, 239.

  Hall, 218.

Recorder, fee to, on surrender, 54.

Recovery of apprentice, 135.

Recreation, 160.

Refusal to serve office, 109.

Release for libel, 119.

Relief of stewards, 124.

Religious services, 173.

Renter Warden, 115.

  accounts of, 116.

  bond of, 115.

  duties of, 115.

Renter Warden, expulsion of, 115.

Resolution of thanks, 240.

Restoration, the, 171.

Reversion to clerkship, 141.

Rich, Geo. Wm., 225, 231.
Richard II, 45.
  confirms Charter, 45.
Right of search, 66.
  procedure as to, 71.
Riot in Henry VIII's reign, 84.
Robbery by clerk, 143.
Robiant, Lawrence, Gift of, 120.
  will of, 41.
Rockingham, Earl of, 101.
Romance of the Rose, 13.
Romney Marsh, 247.
Rope girdles, 10.
Roset and Tirlet, 63.
Royal: Commissions, 201.
  contract, 184.
  proclamations, 92.
  progresses, 169.
Rump Song, 16.
Rushes, 157.
Russian Ambassador, 173.
Rydells destroyed, 178.
Ryley, Mr., 228.

Sack, 159.
Saddle of pork, 156.
Saddlers' Company, 65.
Saint: Bride's, 246.
  John the Baptist, Girdle of, 8.
  Lawrence, 21, 23.
    account of, 23.
  Jewry, 24.

Saint Lawrence: martyrdom of, 23.
  Order of, 21.
  relics of, 23.
  Mark, 8.
  Matthew, 8.
  Michael's, Coventry, 251.
  Paul's Church, 174.
    services at, 174.
  Peter, 22.
  Polycarp's girdle, 9.
Salary: of beadle, 145.
  of clerk, 143.
Salisbury, Mayor of, 66.
Salle, Stephen, steals girdles 19.
Sample girdles, 87.
Saxon: girdles, 9.
  guilds, 24.
Scholarship, girdlers', 251.
Screen, 221.
Sea coal, 180.
Seal, Company's, 45.
Sealers, presentation of, 73.
Sealing, Fees for, 73.
Search, 72.
  artizans' powers, 90.
  right of, 70, 94.
Searchers and Sealers, 71.
Seinturer, 29.
Seizure, Counsel's opinion as to, 92.
Seizure of girdles, 107.
Sequestration of Company, 190.
Sermon, 162, 235.

INDEX

Setting women to work, 90.
Sherborne Lane, 217, 239.
Sheriff made Master, 110.
Ship money, 185.
Sidney's Charity, 247.
Silk girdle, 13.
Silver girdle, 14, 67.
Small beere, 200.
Smiley, Robert, 229.
Smoking, 158.
Smyth, Simon, 55.
Soames, Sir Stephen, 113.
Society of Antiquaries, 44.
Sotherby, James, 220.
Spartan marriage custom, 18.
Spoon, 128.
   money, 128, 193.
Staff: of beadle, 146.
   of porter, 146.
Stamp on Freedom imposed, 128.
Stands, Company's, 169.
Starre Chamber, 96.
Stewards, 120.
   affidavit by, 122.
   fine for not serving, 121.
   fine, reduction of, 123, 124.
   gift to, 120, 235.
   recalcitrant, 122.
   relief of, 124.
   summoned before Lord Mayor, 121.
Stikeneye's case, 70.
Stone, Sir Benjamin, M.P., 165.

Stothard's " Monumental Effigies," 4.
Stow's "London," 33, 209.
Strawberry Ground, 246.
Strutt's " Regal Antiquities," 14.
Strype's remarks as to Girdlers, 22.
Stuart girdles, 16.
Sturgeon, 153.
Subscribing the Test, 55.
Sugar loaf, 159.
Summons to Livery, 125.
Sumptuary Laws, 11, 69.
Sundial, 228.
Suppers, 166.
Surrender: of Charter, 53.
   delivery of, 55.
   of girdle, 18.
Surveyor, 144.
   fee to, 144, 214.
Sutton, Sir Thomas, 114.
Symonds, John, 145.

Tables, 220.
Tavern meetings, 166.
Taylor, Ed., 97, 223.
   Mr., 97.
   speech of Edward, 97.
   Wm., accusation of, 118.
Taxes, 198.
Temple, Mary, 128.
Tenys Balles imported, 83.
Text girdle, 13.
Theft of girdle, 19.

INDEX

Thynne's poem, 16.
Title of Company, 34.
Toasts, 155.
Trade Ordinances, 263.
Tradition as to foundation, 21.
Trained Bands, 198.
Translation: of Charter, 42.
 member, 131.
Travelling expenses, 199.
Treaty of peace, 97.
Trophy tax, 198.
Tudor girdles, 15.
Tussauds, Madame, 6.
Tynbasse, use of, sanctioned, 70.

Ulysses, 7.
Ushers, 139.

Valuation of Hall, 190.
Velvet girdle, 15.
Virginia Company, 182.
Visit to almshouses, 237.
Vote of thanks to Master, 112.

Walls, City, 187.
Walsh's proposal, 129.
Warden Street, complaint of, 118.
Wardens, 106.
 badges of, 112.
 crowning of, 106
 declaration of, 106.
 election of, 106.
 fine for not serving as, 109.
 Renter, 115.

Wardens: substitutes, 138.
Ware, John, 248.
Washing, Company's, 230.
Watchett cloth, 171.
Water Rate, 195.
Watkins, Thomas, 239.
Watt, Richard, complaint of, 136.
Wax tapers provided, 208.
Weeding, T. W., 251.
Welch's charity, 247.
Whifflers, 139, 170.
 duties of, 139.
Whisper, Master chosen by, 106.
White girdle, 20.
White thread girdle, 18.
Wickens, Master, 232.
Widdowes pensions, 196.
Widows fined, 87.
Wildney, accusation of, 117.
William the Conqueror's Charter, 27.
Windebank, Secretary, 50.
Window: stained glass, 212, 220.
 tax, 198.
Wine at dinner, 154.
Wireworkers, 76.
 incorporation of, 48.
 joined to Company, 47.
"Wit Restored," poem, 61.
Woman made free, 128.
Woodthorpe, Mr., 231.
Worshipful Master, 104.

INDEX

Wren, Christopher, 221.
Wyet, Mysteris, 212.

Xenophon, 8.

Yearly feasts, 152
Yellow girdle, 13.
Yeomanry, 100.
  appointment of, 100.

Yeomanry: encouragement of,
  139.
  searchers, 138.

Zeynturer, 178.
Zonam perdere, meaning of,
  18.
Zonar, 29, 178.

CHISWICK PRESS : PRINTED BY CHARLES WHITTINGHAM AND CO.
TOOKS COURT, CHANCERY LANE, LONDON.

ND - #0028 - 100822 - C0 - 229/152/16 - PB - 9781331612872 - Gloss Lamination